A Lighthouse Notebook

ROCKSHORE WADERS
Coquet Island
January

Purple Sandpipers

Redshank

Turnstones

A
LIGHTHOUSE
NOTEBOOK

NORMAN McCANCH

Foreword by Susan Hill

MICHAEL JOSEPH
LONDON

To Monica

MICHAEL JOSEPH LTD

Published by the Penguin Group
27 Wrights Lane, London W8 5TZ, England
Viking Penguin Inc., 40 West 23rd Street, New York, New York 10010, USA
Penguin Books Australia Ltd, Ringwood, Victoria, Australia
Penguin Books Canada Ltd, 2801 John Street, Markham, Ontario, Canada L3R 1B4
Penguin Books (NZ) Ltd, 182-190 Wairau Road, Auckland 10, New Zealand

Penguin Books Ltd, Registered Offices: Harmondsworth, Middlesex, England

First published by Michael Joseph 1985
This paperback edition 1988

Copyright © Norman McCanch, 1985
Introduction copyright © Susan Hill, 1988

Printed and bound in Spain by Artes Gráficas Toledo, S.A.

British Library Cataloguing in Publication Data
Norman McCanch
A lighthouse notebook.
1. Nh—England
I. Title
574.942   QH138.A1

ISBN 0–7181–2688–2
D. L. TO:2260 -1987

CONTENTS

	page
Foreword	7
Introduction	9
How I Came to be There	12
Lighthouse Routines	15
COQUET	25
ST MARY'S ISLAND	51
CROMER	71
SOUTH BISHOP	93
LONGSHIPS	179
Postscript	197
Index	198

Acknowledgements

My thanks are due to all the Lightkeepers who tolerated my enthusiasm and interest in natural history, particularly Pete Smith, who caught the birding bug and continued watching on South Bishop after my departure.

Trinity House kindly gave their approval to my project, and supplied much useful background information on the history of the stations on which I served.

Jenny Dereham, Clare Coney and Susan McIntyre at Michael Joseph Limited gave freely of criticism, encouragement and advice, which made my work much easier.

Undoubtedly my sincerest thanks go to Monica, my wife, who read every word, criticised artwork and text with great perception, and typed all the rough drafts and manuscript unaided. Without her help and encouragement this book would not have been written.

N.V. McCanch

Foreword

by Susan Hill

I was born by the sea and spent my childhood within the sight and sound of it. That was in Yorkshire, and the bleak north-east coast, and so my earliest memories are of gales blowing around the house, high waves crashing up against the cliffs, the sound of the foghorn, the boom of the Lifeboat maroon. And the strangely comforting winking warning light from the lighthouse beacon.

Lighthouses have always seemed to me mildly romantic things, and the charm of living in round rooms must be considerable – no wonder there is always a waiting list of prospective buyers when lighthouses go out of service and up for sale.

Other people's jobs, especially such a rare and unusual job as that of a lighthouse keeper, are a source of endless fascination. If you have ever longed to know just how much food they need to take on to an offshore lighthouse to last a turn of duty, and what *kind* of food, how they get their letters – if they do – and if they play chess or Monopoly in their spare time, and what other curious hobbies might the keepers have, you will find out from A LIGHTHOUSE NOTEBOOK. It is a complete portrait of a way of life in all its professional and domestic detail. Norman McCanch has answered all those questions we would ask him if we had him in front of us in person, and probably all the questions lighthouse keepers are always asked if ever they give talks to Women's Institutes!

But he had a particular interest during his lighthouse years. He was a naturalist, more particularly a bird man – a student of bird migration patterns. What better opportunity to study these at length and undisturbed for weeks and months on end than to be on duty in a lighthouse? Norman McCanch's accounts of what he saw, like his lovely watercolour and pen-and-ink sketches, are meticulously detailed and accurate, but they are full of feeling too. He may have trained as a taxidermist and be scientific in his anatomical approach to the study of bird life; but his delight in and love for the birds he sees are always evident. You do not have to know anything about birds to enjoy this book – you will learn from a very knowledgeable teacher. But if you *do* know something about them, Norman McCanch will enhance your pleasure in bird life and add to the information store of even the most experienced birder.

He also makes us really feel what it is like to be marooned in a lighthouse during winter storms, to appreciate the beauty of dawn and dusk, the play of sunlight and moonlight on the water, and the ever-changing face of the sea. He writes, as it were, 'plain and not fancy', and yet he has the descriptive and evocative skills usually associated with novelists and poets rather than with naturalists and diarists. His book makes you long to get up and go – to the sea, to the shore, to live in a lighthouse, feel the spray in your face, smell the salt air, hear the sea birds' cries.

And A LIGHTHOUSE NOTEBOOK is even more valuable now than when it was first published, because Norman McCanch recorded a world that was changing and, in some respects, dying. The rôle of the lighthouse keeper has become a diminishing one as more and more lighthouses become fully automated and so unmanned. Of those lighthouses he writes about, only Coquet and Longships are still fully manned in the way he describes. Saint Mary's has gone altogether, South Bishop is automated and Cromer partly so.

There will always be the need for the lighthouse beacons to shine out as a warning from around our island, but for how long will lighthouse keepers be needed at all? For those who love the sea and the coastal landscape, the wind and weather, the life of birds and the romantic idea of the lighthouse keeper alone in his turret at the top of a slender white column, this is indeed the perfect book.

Susan Hill
September 1987

INTRODUCTION

A springtime new moon sets early over the Pembrokeshire coast, leaving an enveloping blackness to the night sky which makes every pinpoint of starlight that much brighter. The navigation lights of passing ships are visible for a greater distance than under even a partial moon, and the sweeping arms of light from the Smalls Lighthouse are crisply white against the black horizon. Eastwards from South Bishop the dark mass of Ramsey Island is silhouetted against the glow from St David's beyond, while south-east across St Bride's Bay the street lights of Broad Haven are visible over fourteen miles away. Strumble Head, twenty-five miles north-east, is clearly visible, while on the darkest of nights the loom of Tusker Rock Lighthouse is discernible, even though the light itself, some five miles off the Irish coast and almost forty miles away, is lost below the horizon.

Late April and early May is the peak period for spring migration northwards across the Irish Sea, although on a clear evening there would be little indication of the great movements overhead – possibly the rippling trill of a passing whimbrel, or the sad calling of a curlew flock, drifting down the wind to be heard by a lightkeeper on watch. Even a small change in the weather, however, can produce dramatic evidence of the scale of the journeyings, and the hazards encountered by the small birds involved.

The first indication might be a dulling of the Smalls Lighthouse – yellow where it had formerly been white. In a little while it would change to orange and become a sluggish blip, with no sign of the grandly sweeping beams so noticeable before. The stars would fade behind ragged patches of blackness, until mist obscured the heavens completely, and very shortly after drizzle might begin to dampen the lighthouse walls and glazing. It probably wouldn't be bad enough to sound the fog signal. Smalls would still be visible as a dull red blip to the south-west, while a ship passing south through the St George's Channel would show a red port light visible at a distance of four or five miles.

The beams of the lantern above are thicker now, showing wisps of mist and drizzle, and occasionally illuminating the white underbelly of a Manx shearwater as it flips past the light, filling the sodden air with its own chortling cackle. Odd wader calls come down the wind, hoarse dunlin flocks 'schreeping' as they pass, whimbrel and curlew, possibly a group of noisy godwits drifting northwards. They seldom come into the beams of light on South Bishop, preferring to pass close by unseen.

Then, without warning, a small brilliantly-lit shape dances momentarily in the beams of the light and is gone. Gradually another appears, and a couple more, until perhaps twenty or thirty small warblers and chats are flickering in the dazzling light. Unable to pinpoint any other landmark in the drizzle and mist, they fly towards the light, circling in its beams until exhaustion or daybreak frees them. Some flutter at the glazing, others crash into the glass or aerial wires and are killed, their tiny bodies falling into the yard and guttering. Many call in their confusion, and even snatches of full song are heard as a displacement activity.

I take a small hand net onto the gallery of the lantern and crouch below the light, watching the flickering shapes, trying to estimate the numbers and identify the odd calls and cheeps. Circling the gallery I find the warm corpse of a sedge warbler lying on the floor. As I put it in a box for later examination I hear a bump above me, and a fluttering along the glazing. I see a bird which looks enormous and brilliant white in the glare from the light, crouching against the window ledge, panting. A flick of the net catches a fine male wheatear, which is quickly put into the safety of a cloth bag for ringing and release at dawn. Other birds are about now, wheatears, sedge and willow warblers, a tiny goldcrest which flutters into me as I crouch in the darkness, and settles down to sleep on my arm. I try to catch all that come to the light but occasionally I hear a bump as one crashes against the glass. I catch up four or five more, including a couple of whitethroats, and take them down the tower to roost in the cool storeroom. As I return across the yard I find tiny corpses of warblers lying below the aerial wire. A loud crash followed by a heavy thump indicates an unplanned landing by a Manx shearwater and I hurry to find him, sitting dazed and confused in the middle of the yard. Shearwaters are as tough as nails, and I gather him up into a cardboard box, to let him recover in safety. It begins to drizzle more heavily now as I stand steaming from the unaccustomed exercise of trying to catch up the living, collect the dead, and occasionally destroy the horribly maimed. The tiny willow warblers and chiffchaffs have natural predators to contend with, too, for suddenly the great shape of a short-eared owl drifts through the beam to snatch a small warbler in flight. The tiny bird squeals and is silent, and the owl settles on a rock to swallow his prey. Twice more this happens, but my attempts to catch the owl are fruitless. More shearwaters dash past now, and one or two misjudge the light and fall into the yard, to be caught for ringing. They peck and struggle, leaving me with scratches and lacerations on fingers and hands.

I switch on the house lights which illuminate the yard but leave patches of deep shadow in odd corners. This brings birds down from the gallery to land on the window ledges, safe from the dangers of collision. They soon drift into the darker corners and settle down to sleep, enabling me to catch a few more, including three or four meadow pipits, phlegmatic birds well able to cope with lighthouses.

Gradually the blackness fades to grey, and as dawn comes the attraction fizzles out, birds finding safe perches among the gantries and rigging below them. Daylight is the time for reckoning – twenty or thirty corpses recovered, mostly sedge warblers, but also a spotted flycatcher and a grasshopper warbler. None of these wears a ring, but all will be examined for parasites and preserved for museum specimens. There are perhaps eighteen to twenty birds to be ringed, sexed, aged, measured and weighed. All are carefully examined for signs of any injury sustained the night before, and only if fully fit are they ringed and released.

The shearwaters fly off strongly, doubtless with a sick headache, launched from the cliff edge so that the waiting gulls, already scavenging corpses floating off-shore, have no chance to intercept them. All around the island redstarts, wheatears, flycatchers and warblers are hunting insects among the sparse vegetation. Occasionally a chiffchaff sings from an aerial wire, the breath of the British woodland brought to this barren rock. He probably realises that the last major hazard of his journey from West Africa is past and he won't have to face similar ones again for at least four months. In the next day or so he moves on, the short hop to take up his territory for the summer is nothing by comparison with the miles covered in the past few days.

HOW I CAME TO BE THERE

Purley Grammar School sweltered in the first heatwave of spring, while out on the rugby pitch I could see a little group of lesser black-backed gulls searching the grass for scraps left by untidy schoolboys. In a non-maritime county like Surrey, these gulls moving north with the spring were like a lifeline to my earlier childhood on the Welsh coast and as they lifted from the field and drifted away over the rooftops, I longed to follow them.

The careers master shuffled his bits of paper and glanced briefly at me. I knew that he was rapidly going through a resumé of my limited academic achievements and the endless 'could do better' comments of my teachers, trying to find some clue to my character. After six years at the school this was the first time we had sat face to face. He was a capable teacher of mathematics and physics, subjects I was unable to comprehend even the need for studying, and so our paths had not crossed until now. 'Well, McCanch,' he said, 'what do you want to do when you leave school?' His tone was encouraging, even comradely, a sort of 'let's get together man-to-man and sort this out' no-nonsense approach. He winced visibly at my reply, 'I want to be a taxidermist, or a lighthouse keeper, or even warden of a nature reserve.' He shuffled some more bits of paper and scrutinised one closely at some length before thrusting it at me saying: 'Here's an interesting job, McCanch, Patents Officer! Ever thought of being a Patents Officer? Take this away and tell me what you think next week!'

I left, dutifully clutching the printed information sheet, pausing only to see who was next in the queue. The careers master would get on well with him, a boy I vaguely knew whose only ambition was to be the greatest living expert on Foreign Exchange. The information sheet, printed on crisp, high-quality, Her Majesty's Stationery Office paper, later held that summer's record for the longest straight-line flight of a delta-wing design paper aeroplane.

The following week at the appointed time I sneaked into the Senior Biology Lab to skin a dead gull found on a field trip over the weekend.

Later in the summer I wrote to a firm of taxidermists in London, asking for a job. I was called for an interview, took a few examples of my work along, and was offered a position as a trainee, commencing as soon as I left school.

In September 1972 I began working for Rowland Ward Ltd, the oldest established firm of taxidermists in the world. The great bulk of the work handled was African big game, and the opportunities it gave for the close study of unusual creatures was unparalleled in my experience. Taxidermy is a much neglected art form which requires considerable knowledge of anatomy, movement and behaviour of the creatures involved, as well as a wide range of manual skills to cope with everything from skinning and sewing to woodwork and painting. The understanding of animal structure it gives is without equal. Only someone who has skinned a lion's foot can appreciate the intricate mass of muscles and tendons which control even a relatively simple action like retraction of the claws, and every animal is a vast complex of inter-linked working parts.

While learning my trade I collected many specimens for my own study and kept notebooks and simple sketches of animals both alive and dead. Eventually, drawing animals and birds became an end in itself, rather than simply an extension of my interest in taxidermy, and I started to use my collection of bird skins for artistic reference in a different field. I shared a flat with two other taxidermists which was an amazing hotch-potch of bits of bone and feathers, skins, shells and drawings, so that we lived surrounded by, and totally absorbed in, the things we felt to be important. After a couple of years, however, living in London began to lose its appeal, so that when my period of training at Rowland Ward came to an end, I looked around for an opportunity to return to the rural life I missed, which I now realised was important to me.

Birds were my real obsession and in my late teens I had qualified for a ringing licence, and become increasingly fascinated by migration studies. I had read the accounts of several Victorian naturalists, but the work of one man in particular had caught my imagination. Heinrich Gätke had lived on the island of Heligoland in the nineteenth century, and had devoted his life to the study and collection of migrant birds. His descriptions of lighthouse attractions sparked a desire in me to witness them at first hand.

The opportunity came about in an odd way. I was working on a temporary job with the Metropolitan Water Board, digging silt from the bed of a canal under a road bridge at Ware in Hertfordshire. In my lunchtime I sat on the grassy banks of the canal, eating my sandwiches and wondering how to get the job of the chap who mowed the grass over the entire ten-mile stretch. It seemed an infinitely more pleasant occupation on a warm summer afternoon. When we talked, I discovered he had worked on lightships, before the frustration of remaining firmly anchored in one place while ships passed on their way to exotic locations had persuaded him to join a tanker fleet and sail the world. I pressed him further, until he suggested I write to Trinity House at Tower Hill in London and try my luck.

Coincidence no doubt, but my enquiry about employment was made at a time when the Lighthouse Service was undergoing a radical alteration of structure, aimed at providing duplicate crews for each rock light. Recruitment was underway and in less than three weeks I had been accepted, had passed a medical and had gone home to Pembrokeshire to await my first instructions.

When they arrived shortly after, they were characteristically to the point: ATTEND FOUR WEEKS INITIAL TRAINING COURSE TRINITY HOUSE WORKSHOPS LEAMOUTH ROAD, BLACKWALL COMMENCING MONDAY NEXT 1000 HOURS. So back to London, albeit temporarily, I went!

LIGHTHOUSE ROUTINES

Lighthouses work efficiently largely because of well-tried routines which are flexible enough to allow for the unexpected. There are two main systems for dividing up the day's duties between the three keepers stationed on a rock light. The first is straightforward, giving each man eight hours of duty every day for the full twenty-eight day tour. The watches run from four a.m. to midday (morning watch), midday to eight p.m. (afternoon) and a split shift covering midnight to four a.m. (middle) and eight p.m. to midnight (evening). This split shift is to allow for a Trinity House ruling that no keeper be on watch for more than four hours during darkness.

The second system uses the same basic watches, but the morning (four a.m. to midday) and evening (eight p.m. to midnight) are done by the same man, which gives each keeper twenty-four hours free of duty after a middle watch. This system is particularly popular on island lighthouses, but when you have nowhere to go, a day off isn't quite so appealing! Of the rock lights I worked on, South Bishop used the former system while Coquet and Longships used the latter.

The basic household chores are the responsibility of the keeper on morning watch, in addition to the normal routine tasks of watch keeping. His day begins just after four a.m. when the middle watchman gives him a call. It is surprising how quickly one's body becomes accustomed to the routine, a tap on the door and switching on the light being sufficient to bring him down into the living room in a few minutes. The kettle has boiled and over an early-morning cup of tea the details and events of the watch just gone are passed from one man to the other. The state of the weather, particularly visibility and wind, the state of the sea, any shipping forecasts or gale warnings received and any details of generators and light gear which may need special attention, are of importance to the man on watch. This small ritual of 'handing over the watch' is important, it makes plain to both men at which point responsibility is passed from one to the other and prevents misunderstanding about who is actually on watch.

The middle watchman is quickly off to bed, and after a second cup of tea, the day's domestic duties begin. The living accommodation is swept and mopped daily, through the bathroom, kitchen and radio room to the living room. Shelves and window ledges are wiped over too, although there isn't a lot of dust, it doesn't get a chance to settle! Each day had a specific morning watch task, a chore done only once a week, perhaps cleaning windows or mopping down the tower stairs, while washing the lantern glazing is a twice-weekly task and in bad weather with much sea spray it may be done more frequently.

People imagine that lighthouse routines involve endless cleaning, but lightkeepers keep this to the minimum required for efficiency and hygiene and become adept at finding ways around it. On Longships the steep galvanised stairways have a hand-slot in each tread, and gleaming brass hand-rails up each side. These are polished once a week, and rigorously avoided at all other times except in an emergency. It is far safer and more convenient to use the hand-slot.

After breakfast the generator is switched over and the out-going one is cleaned and wiped down in readiness for its next use. There are three generators available, and they are run in turn for twenty-four hours at a stretch. There may be a small maintenance task to carry out in the engine room, changing an oil filter or putting batteries on charge, and we usually mop over the red tile floor with a special detergent to clean up any slippery oil spots which may be hazardous in an emergency.

Every three hours the state of weather is entered in the log book, an accurate recording of wind direction and speed, state of the weather and barometer readings, signed after each entry by the keeper on watch and available as an independent and unbiased record of the weather conditions prevailing in the event of an accident to shipping and a subsequent inquiry.

Twice a day, just after nine a.m. and two p.m., there is a radio check. Lighthouses are gathered into radio groups, each group using a local frequency. At these times a coastguard calls up every station in turn, to give a test of radio transmission and reception. It also provides an opportunity to make contact with other keepers, if only briefly. The compulsory silence periods on the hour and half-hour are listened to for any indication of distress locally, and just after these finish is the time you may receive radio messages through a G.P.O. coast radio station, or from a lighthouse tender. Each lighthouse also has a speaker permanently tuned to the international calling and distress frequency 2182 kHz, which cannot be turned off.

Apart from cooking breakfast the most important morning job is putting out the light. Times of lighting up and extinguishing are set out in tables based on the seasonal lengthening and shortening of daylight, with the provision for lighting up earlier in poor visibility, but the actual time of extinguishing (on South Bishop) will vary from about four-forty a.m. in summer to eight-thirty a.m. in winter. The job itself is simple in the case of an electric light, more elaborate with an oil burner, requiring considerable time to be spent cleaning the lamp in readiness for its next use. Not to be overlooked is the hanging of the gallery curtains, which may be fifteen feet high in some cases, as at St Mary's Island. These prevent the sun's rays being focused by the lense onto the bulb or burner, for the heat generated would be sufficient to melt the metal parts on a bright sunny day.

One of the nicest aspects of the morning watch is being completely alone for six hours, particularly when there is an impressive dawn to sit and watch. But between ten and ten-thirty the two off-watch keepers get up for breakfast and then comes the opportunity to tackle any of those jobs which may require two or three men.

Pumping water into header tanks is a job made easier by an extra pair of hands, while maintaining ropes, routine repairs to buildings and greasing-up gantries, winch-cables and aerial ropeways all have to be done on a monthly basis. During the summer months the boat landings and steps need lime-washing every couple of weeks to prevent the growth of algae and seaweed, which make the footings slippery and treacherous, although rough weather can delay the task even in summer.

When a lighthouse tender arrives off station to deliver stores, all three keepers are required to carry out the transfer safely. On South Bishop I had the job of winch driver. A glass and metal control box on the cliff edge gave me an excellent view of all the proceedings in the boat landing sixty feet below. The other keepers work on the boat landings, throwing mooring ropes to hold the launch while stores are lifted clear and one man then climbs the steep steps to the gantry to free the cargo net from the winch cable. On a major delivery of oil or water some of the tender's crew come on station to assist, as the transfer may take two or three hours, and then the atmosphere becomes almost party-like, with old newspapers and endless communal pots of tea.

Land lights have slightly different routines, for although the basic watches are the same, St Mary's Island, for example, doesn't have a fog signal and consequently there is a provision that all keepers may be absent from the station from eleven a.m. to one hour before the light goes in, generally three-thirty p.m. at the time of year I was there. Cromer was open to the public from one p.m. to one hour before lighting up, always by arrangement with the keeper on watch. His agreement is important, for after every group of visitors the tower has to be washed down again, so that dirty footprints don't have a chance to accumulate. Most of the visitors at Cromer were school parties, generally as part of a special project, and they were always keen to ask questions and collect pamphlets and publications. Many of the adults were less perceptive, however, and at St Mary's Island the 120-foot tower daunted some, who asked to use the lift, and couldn't believe that a ten-minute walk up stairs, and a slightly quicker one down, was the only way to do it!

Food and Other Supplies

The food a keeper eats on a lighthouse is his own responsibility. He receives a victualling allowance towards the cost of it, but the choice and the physical aspects of gathering it are left entirely to him.

What you actually choose to take is governed to some extent by the nature of the lighthouse you are going to. A tower light such as Longships has limited space for the storage of frozen food, so we tended to subsist on a diet of sausages or bacon with various permutations of vegetables and onion gravy, only having chops or chicken portions in the first week of a tour of duty. The cramped facilities meant that the morning watchman cooked the midday meal for all three keepers and as a consequence the cook tended to stick to something safe in the vegetable line, each man leaving the meat of his choice in the kitchen the night before, and the cook having the run of a communal 'pool' of fresh vegetables.

Coquet and South Bishop, with more spacious accommodation, allowed each man to cook for himself and, incidentally, to do his washing up straight away afterwards! On Coquet I was new to the art of lighthouse cookery, but by the time I arrived on South Bishop I had gained some experience of my own likes and dislikes, and found plenty of ways to pamper my taste-buds while on duty!

South Bishop had excellent facilities for the storage of food, each man having a large cupboard in the larder, a full-size refrigerator and ample space in his bedroom for the storage of tinned food if necessary. Limitations on what you took were largely a result of the helicopter transport, where the pay-load was strictly limited, giving each man a rucksack and holdall for personal gear, a laundry bag and four food boxes, each measuring three feet by two feet by eighteen inches deep and made of high-impact plastic, which effectively protected the food inside.

No restriction was placed on taking alcohol on station, but it would occupy space in food boxes and each man had to decide for himself which was most desirable. During my service on South Bishop our crew only took alcohol at Christmas, although the Principal Keeper on the other watch actually carried on his hobby of wine-making on station, while the keepers on nearby Skokholm, with the advantage of a bird observatory on the island with regular boat services, went in for beer-making in quite a serious way. Smokers, likewise, had to consider their consumption of tobacco carefully, and take sufficient with them to last a full month. My first crew on Coquet, and also on Longships, was made up entirely of non-smokers, a situation much to our liking but not common. On the whole keepers who smoked showed some consideration for non-smokers, and certainly cleaned their own ashtrays!

Paraffin or gas fridges and Calor gas cookers are usual on rock lighthouses, although Longships had a huge oil-fired range which required much forward planning and patience to cook a meal, and which never quite got the heat up to fry chips, so we normally ate our potatoes roasted, baked or boiled. A paraffin fridge, no matter how unlikely it sounds, is a simple and very efficient object only requiring the wick to be cleaned and trimmed when it is filled twice a week (by the morning watchman, as a regular chore). As the month progresses, it is usual to use one fridge for the decreasing amount of frozen food, and shut the others down to save fuel. They would be cleaned thoroughly and re-lit just before relief to provide the incoming crew with fridges ready to receive their perishable goods.

So what do you take? It depends on what you like but as a general rule my food list for twenty-eight days on South Bishop would be rather as follows.

About three dozen tins, containing vegetables, fruit, meat, fish and condensed milk. Although bulky and rather heavy, tins are an absolute must – most keepers permanently attached to a station build up a small stock of tins as a personal emergency supply, although it sometimes comes about as a result of finding something unappetising. Tinned fish, for instance, often remains unopened in summer when mackerel and pollack are catchable, but is very useful during winter storms and overdues.

Dry goods included sugar, flour, rice and biscuits. They were usually repacked in extra polythene bags and taped up to keep out the damp. These goods tended to be used up in one tour as they deteriorate once open. They would normally be boxed up with the tins and packed in with newspaper or towels and clothing to stop them rattling about. Condiments and sauces tended to accumulate as it was very difficult to remember how much was actually on station and it was better to play safe than sorry! Coffee, tea, marmalade, jams and sweets also had to be found room for.

Perishable goods included frozen chicken, duck, mince, sausages, bacon, eggs, cheese, butter, bread and longlife milk. Basically these were kept either frozen or chilled. Meat was deep frozen at home for a week or so before relief day, and then packed in thick layers of foil and newspaper for the journey. Most arrived on station in a fair state, and I never suffered with food poisoning from those which had thawed a little! Chicken and duck, once cooked, were generally eaten as main meals on four consecutive days, usually in the first and second weeks. Mince and stewing steak would be portioned up into four-ounce lots before freezing, to prevent the need to defrost the whole with disastrous results. Eggs, bacon and cheese would all be stored in the cool part of the fridge, but loaves of sliced bread fared better being kept frozen and thawed out a few slices at a time when needed. This prevented the bread drying out and helped spread the three loaves over about two weeks. Once this had gone, home-made bread would have to be eaten rather more quickly, and so by the end of the month crispbread would have to be resorted to!

Fresh fruit and vegetables, totalling about forty-five pounds in weight, were stored in open wire or plastic racks in a cool dark storeroom. All fresh fruit and vegetables seemed to keep well on lighthouses although tomatoes and green peppers had a limited lifespan, and had to be kept in the bottom of the fridge. For some reason I never quite understood, I always seemed to have potatoes left over. I started my lightkeeping career taking twenty-eight pounds for a month, dropped it to fourteen pounds and then only ten pounds, but still had a few left after every tour of duty. It was a good idea to check them every couple of days to rub off any new sprouts, but otherwise they kept well.

Compulsive eating must be regarded as an occupational hazard in lightkeeping. It is very appealing to eat sandwiches and snacks in the middle of the night and most keepers eat a substantial main meal. Some degree of self-discipline is necessary and in my case this included only eating bacon and eggs (a favourite) when on morning watch, after the domestic chores had been finished!

Tea and coffee drinking also becomes a compulsion, particularly as no one on South Bishop would make tea or coffee without offering some to the other two almost as a ritual; invariably it was impossible not to accept. The social implications of sharing tea and coffee among lightkeepers would be a fruitful field for sociological study!

As a safety margin, each light has a supply of basic emergency rations to cope with overdues or accidents. These are in the charge of the Principal Keeper, and he has a checklist for their issue. They have to be paid for, but that isn't important when the alternative is to go without. They even include a ration of cigarettes for those in desperate need! The only occasion on which I needed them was on South Bishop when I left all my butter and fats ashore, and had to buy a tin of butter to last me until my own was kindly delivered by a Royal Navy Survey vessel, which landed on the rock to fix up a temporary radar reflector.

All other stores, such as water, fuel oil, gas, engine parts, cleaning materials, toilet rolls, etc., are delivered by lighthouse tender. The west-coast tender which served South Bishop was the Trinity House Vessel *Winston Churchill*, based at the Swansea Depot, and she arrived off station generally once a month, weather permitting, to land general supplies, oil and water. Fuel oil was usually winched onto the crane gantry in forty-five gallon drums, and then pumped direct into three 1,500 gallon tanks, the empties being returned straight away in a cargo net. Drinking water usually arrived in vast 300-gallon tanks, and these remained in the launch moored at the boat landing, to be pumped direct into the storage tanks. In addition, rain water was collected from the roof at South Bishop, and run into separate tanks to be used for domestic washing purposes. Even so, during the drought of 1976 it became necessary to use sea water, collected by means of an oil drum on the winch cable, for flushing the lavatory. On tower lights such as Longships, washing-up water was collected in buckets after use, so that it could be used for the same purpose!

Hobbies and Free Time

Even allowing for watchkeeping duties and routine chores, keepers are left with a considerable amount of free time on station which has to be filled.

Radio and television help in keeping you in touch with the outside world, although reception can be poor in prolonged bad weather, and it is difficult to watch the news without a strange feeling of detachment from reality.

Reading is almost a way of life, all the offshore stations I served on had a large store of paperbacks and magazines, keepers tended to bring books from home and the atmosphere on a lighthouse was well suited to working through mighty and improving tomes which would gladden the heart of any English teacher. Certainly I had never got far with *Seven Pillars of Wisdom* until I took it to South Bishop.

Card and board games are not so popular, they rather depend on finding someone to play with, and it is infuriating to teach a novice how to play Scrabble at the beginning of the month, only to have him beat you by increasingly large margins by the time you are due to leave. I fared rather better with chess, as I had not won a game since the fifth form at school, and so had no honour to defend. I have seen serious arguments erupt over Monopoly and Scrabble, and fortunes in matches amassed at poker and rummy, so it isn't all that surprising that most keepers have some interest which is carried on at a solitary level. Model-making is common, either from plastic kits or balsa wood, while some keepers are skilled in the secret art of putting ships in bottles. Painting, both in oils and watercolour, is also popular, while one keeper who had formerly been a journalist worked steadily at serious writing. Wine and beer-making, building up a suntan, fishing and making fishing tackle, photography and music all had their place. A varied range of instruments from clarinets to guitars appeared from time to time, while one of the keepers on St Mary's Island had been a canoe instructor and kept a kayak on the beach below the tower.

Few of the keepers I served with were interested in natural history, although most were tolerant of my all-consuming passion for it. I kept my detailed logbooks of observations on birds, mammals, insects, fish and even the weather and forwarded these to museums and local Natural History Societies. I made sketches and drawings of things which interested me, collected dead birds, fish and mammals as specimens for museum collections, caught and ringed migrant birds and even collected their parasites for research workers in Cambridge. One keeper on South Bishop was unable to ignore my obsession with birds and eventually bought binoculars and books and became keen enough to take his hobby ashore with him, something which gave me great satisfaction.

People ashore, when told I was a lightkeeper, invariably asked: 'Don't you get terribly bored?' Boredom is entirely a frame of mind, and in my time as a lightkeeper I never once heard a keeper utter those words.

Bird Ringing and Specimen Collecting

Some lighthouses, by virtue of their geographical position and the character of their light, attract migrant birds in large numbers during spring and autumn. As these birds are on passage, it is quite valuable to be able to catch and ring as many individuals as possible, to gather information about their origins and destinations. Ringing is a precise and demanding skill which requires between two and three years part-time training before a novice is permitted to ring unaccompanied, and I was fortunate to have qualified for a full licence during the year in which I joined the Lighthouse Service.

The National Ringing Scheme is administered by the British Trust for Ornithology who supply the rings, equipment and recording forms to registered permit holders. These are by no means free, and any ringer who handles a large number of birds can expect a substantial capital outlay on rings and equipment.

The fitting of the metal rings is done with specially adapted pliers and the details recorded of each bird include ring number, species, sex and age, wing length, weight, time, date and locality of ringing, and any general notes about moult and condition. Re-traps, i.e. birds ringed previously and caught again, have the same details recorded, as much of the valuable information derived by the scheme comes from repeated captures of individuals, sometimes over many years.

Before you can do all this, however, you have to catch your bird! Lighthouses provide two main ways of capture. Birds attracted to the light at night during overcast conditions are disorientated and can be caught either by hand or in a butterfly net, as they flutter against the glazing or doze in sheltered corners. Certainly in the case of birds fluttering about in darkness careful capture and storage overnight in a cloth bag or roost box prevents subsequent injury and often death. When dawn comes these birds can be ringed and released with confidence, although if the occasional one shows signs of being dazed, perhaps by a collision in the dark, such a bird would be released unringed.

To catch birds flitting about the rocks during the day requires the use of a mist net. This is a very fine nylon net which is supported between two bamboo canes. When placed against a suitable background it is practically invisible to birds in flight and they fly into the meshes, to be held safely in a pocket of loose netting, about a foot or so off the ground. A skilled operator can extract them in a few seconds with no harm done and they can quickly be on their way. Wind is the major enemy of mist netters, for the meshes are so fine that they billow in the slightest breeze, making the net easily visible. On South Bishop I used small nets, some three feet high and twenty to thirty feet long, and tried to fit them unobtrusively into sheltered gullies; even so few days were really suitable for netting and the frustrations of trying to catch an unusual bird on a blustery day could drive a ringer to drink.

In the past, museum researchers who wished to add further specimens to their collections simply went out and shot or trapped the creatures they needed, with little thought for the future of the species. In more enlightened times such 'active collecting' is no longer acceptable to the majority of people, and so even major museums ascribe a great deal of importance to specimens gained through 'passive collecting', that is, making use of corpses derived from road casualties, oil-spills or lighthouse attractions. With my training as a taxidermist behind me I paid particular attention to collecting any specimens which came my way, preserving them and passing them on to research workers and institutions. Everything from butterflies and moths to sheep ticks and fleas was of interest to somebody, but while invertebrates could be dried or pickled in surgical alcohol, birds had to be skinned and cured.

Most museums, in addition to mounted specimens on display, have large collections of 'study skins'. These are stuffed birds, but made up in the form of a dead bird lying on its back, with wings closed and legs neatly crossed. A data label containing all relevant information about its origins is tied to its leg and these are the stock-in-trade of museum researchers, for all the details of plumage are preserved and comparisons can be made with other specimens, even down to measuring the relative lengths of adjacent feathers, to determine species and geographical variants. I was able to supply specimens to a number of institutions, particularly Manchester Museum, and also maintain a small collection for my own reference, while for drawings and paintings it was often useful to keep odd feathers or groups of feathers from specimens too badly damaged to preserve intact.

To prepare a study skin is quite straightforward but, like many things, in practice it is a good deal harder than the theory would have you believe. On most birds you begin with a careful incision down the belly, using a very sharp scalpel and then it is largely a matter of peeling the skin away from the body, cutting through the wing, tail and leg joints, before turning the skin completely inside-out, and severing the neck. Then the skull must be freed by peeling the skin gently down towards the beak, freeing the ear and eye attachments and then removing the tongue, eyes and brain. Every scrap of body fat must be cleaned from the skin and then it can be cured using Borax or some other preservative. With the skin turned the right way out again an artificial body of cotton wool or wood straw can be fitted, eye sockets made up with a wisp of cotton wool and the whole sewn up. The body should be dissected and sexed anatomically, and a note made of any stomach or gut contents. Then a data label is written out, attached to the legs and the specimen is left to dry for a week or so. Another useful specimen saved from the process of decomposition.

COQUET ISLAND, NORTHUMBERLAND
55° 20′ N ; 1° 33′ W

COQUET

Coquet Island is situated about a mile offshore from the town of Amble in Northumberland, lying across the mouth of the Coquet River (*Plate* 2). It is small, only about ten acres in extent, composed largely of sandstone capped with thin soil and sparse vegetation, riddled with rabbit burrows. The tallest cliffs on the island are no more than twenty feet high, sloping down to a shallow, sandy beach below the tower at the southern end. At low tide the whole island is surrounded by a sandstone reef broken up into many rock pools, much favoured by waders and seaduck. North-east gales bring saltspray drifting right across the island, scorching the vegetation and making the few freshwater pools weakly saline.

Sandstone was cut on the island as long ago as 1600, and many of the quarrymen carved their names and dates on the low cliff. Although most are now worn and illegible, on one cliff the date 1821 can be made out under a sheltering overhang.

(*Plate* 2)

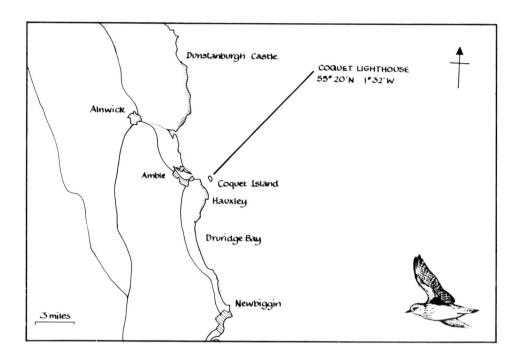

The lighthouse itself was built in 1841 on the vault of an older tower, and incorporates the ruins of an ancient chapel into some of the out-buildings. The oldest part survives as the lighthouse oil store, and was a cell built by a hermit in the seventh century. This room is only about six feet square, and has a small window high up on the south wall, with a heavy iron door shutting off the rest of the lighthouse. There is a step to the window and two paces back again, the longest journey it is possible to make confined in that tiny cell. A footprint worn into the step is the work of a Dutchman who came to the monastery seeking a penance for his sins. The monks locked him in the cell for thirty years, feeding him through a tiny aperture and denying him any contact with his fellow men. He died there, leaving the room with a melancholy and sad atmosphere and certainly no place to linger on a dark night.

The quarrymen and the monks have long since gone, although in these Gothic surroundings it is not difficult to imagine that one monk, in spirit at least, still wanders the landings and galleries. Lay a hand on the annexe door, start to open it and you will feel the unmistakable 'shoving past' of someone in a hurry. It isn't the wind, for it happens in windless conditions; neither is it threatening or in any way malevolent, most likely a young monk so engrossed in fishing that he forgot Vespers and is in a rush to get to prayers. Or just possibly it's a lighthouse keeper's imagination! In any case,

Coquet is now left to the lightkeepers and a National Trust warden during the summer, who watches over the large colonies of breeding terns and eiders.

At the time of my assignment to Coquet, in 1975, only four Trinity House lighthouses had an oil burner as a main navigation light. Coquet was one of those, and I quickly learnt to respect the simplicity of the apparatus which had been the backbone of Victorian navigation aids, and was now being rapidly superseded by electricity.

Imagine a cast-iron burner, surmounted by an incandescent mantle burning vapourised oil just like a tilly lamp, but six times the size! The oil was supplied under pressure from a fuel tank at the base of the tower; this had to be filled with oil from jerry-cans every morning and the pressure (about eighty psi) was supplied by means of a hand pump and plenty of arm muscle every couple of hours. The reason oil burners survived so long was plain to see, with no complex moving parts other than a hand pump and a few brass valves, nothing could go wrong which a patient lightkeeper armed with simple tools, and a few spares and time, could not put right. Modern lights require sophisticated mechanical knowledge to repair and maintain. With an oil light, keepers could do the work themselves. Stripping down the apparatus and thoroughly cleaning it every morning not only kept it in good order but gave advance notice of any worn parts which might need replacement. It also meant that there was no possibility of coming to lighting-up time and finding something in need of cleaning or repair.

Throw a couple of switches and an electric lamp is lit. An oil light requires more planning and patience. At the bottom of the tower you check the fuel tank and pressure vessel, making sure both are full to their optimum level, and that all the right valves are open and the wrong ones closed. Up the tower, to the lantern itself, remove the curtains which protect the lamp from the sun's rays, and climb inside the lens for a strangely distorted view of the world outside. Check that all the valve switches are off, the mantle is not damaged, and that a spare is close at hand. Take a small, circular brass pan, fill it with methylated spirits from a copper flask, ignite it and place under the burner, wait about ten minutes, admire the view and then, when the meths is getting low, check the vaporiser tubes, which by now have a faint reddish glow from the heat of the burning spirit. Turn the feed valve on slightly to allow a small trickle of fuel oil into the burner tubes, where the heat evaporates it into a cloud of white smoke which ignites with a dull pop and hisses orange-red around the mantle. Wait a few minutes more until the mantle itself begins to glow orange and then patchy white, and turn the feed valve slowly up to its fullest extent. The flow of pressurised oil causes the mantle to glow increasingly until it becomes uniformly white-hot, burning with a strong hissing sound. After a minute or so it can only be looked at when wearing dark goggles, but this is necessary to check that the mantle hasn't split under the pressure. If it does, it will probably need replacing during the night.

When the burner is well under way the occulting mechanism, which obscures the light for three seconds in every thirty, is wound up and set in motion, raising and lowering a metal cone over the burning mantle in a regular cycle, driven by a clockwork motor which has to be wound up by hand every hour. Coquet has a fixed lens which doesn't rotate, so the occulter is the only way of making the light give its particular signal.

So the cycle continues throughout the night, the lamp, pressure levels and clockwork drive each requiring to be checked every hour by the keeper on watch until daybreak when it is all ready for cleaning once again.

On 2nd January 1975, I made the crossing to Coquet by local boat, to replace a keeper taken ashore in an emergency. I was to spend the next five weeks on station during which I came across several creatures new to me.

JANUARY 3rd My first full day on a rock lighthouse, the morning was completely taken up by an extended tour of the station during which Geordie, the principal keeper, explained the various routines and equipment relevant to Coquet. Each station differs in some respect with regard to the type of machinery installed, hence the need for a fairly detailed introduction to the eccentricities of a new lighthouse.

After lunch I went out for a look around the island. The previous evening I had noticed large numbers of gulls roosting towards the north end, so I made my way past the boat landing up to the roost site, to see what I could find. Apart from lots of discarded feathers, odd chop-bones and pellets containing bits of paper and plastic, there were one or two old corpses of herring gulls and a fresh first-winter great black-backed gull. Large roosts like this always include sick or injured individuals, very often dying as a result of being shot and wounded during the day. Many of the birds frequent rubbish tips and occasionally one may pick up a dose of rat poison. This first-winter great black-backed gull was in such good condition that I made a reference drawing of its plumage before I prepared it as a study skin. A brief post-mortem did indeed prove it to have been shot.

Evening brings large numbers of gulls to the roost. They start arriving in mid-afternoon, long lines and scattered flocks drifting in from the adjacent coast, and larger groups which have spent the day inland or around the rubbish dumps. The early arrivals often settle in for a bath and preen in the small fresh-water pools on the island, before picking a good position to spend the night. Early arrival doesn't guarantee a prime roost site, however, for young herring gulls give way to older ones, and most of them give way to the larger and much more aggressive great black-backs. As a result the

GLAUCOUS GULLS
Coquet Island
January

Head of 2nd-winter bird
note pale eye and bill tip.

1st-winter bird

(Plate 3)

younger birds tend to congregate at the edges of the flocks, where on a mainland roost they would be more susceptible to ground predators such as foxes and rats.

Quite early in the evening I noticed a stranger arriving from the north with a flock of black-backs. Equally large, but pale buff with clear white wing tips, it was a first-winter glaucous gull, only the second I had ever seen. It settled on the rocks by the boat landing for ten minutes, and dispossessed a herring gull of a dead fish, before flying to the middle of the roosting flock and settling down in a comfortable position unchallenged. Needless to say soon after it had settled it was lost from sight, but not before I had made a few sketches (*Plate 3*). Glaucous gulls are Arctic breeders and small numbers wander to the British coast in winter. They are more frequent in Scotland and on the north-east coast than anywhere else in the British Isles, and I had hoped to find one while I was here.

JANUARY 4th

Eiders were much in evidence this morning, over fifty feeding just offshore from the boat landing. They were diving repeatedly and at least one came up with a green crab. I presume the main attraction to have been shellfish, for when the tide fell I noticed that the rocks in the general vicinity were quite heavily carpeted with good-sized mussels.

Later on I found an oystercatcher wandering about below the garden wall, and caught it without difficulty. It was very thin, its breast-bone sharp and prominent through the feathers. I collected some shellfish from the rocks and force-fed it, but despite eating four or five mussels and a few limpets it showed no improvement and remained standing hunched in the corner of the yard. I made a few sketches (*Plate 4*), but eventually left it in peace. Later in the evening it died, and after adding some reference drawings to my sketches I skinned it and did a quick post-mortem, but didn't find any obvious reason for its sorry state.

JANUARY 5th   Steadily increasing winds during the day, reaching westerly force seven in the mid-afternoon, seemed to adversely effect the wader numbers. I only found one small group of purple sandpipers and turnstones, numbering about twenty, with a single ringed plover and about a dozen oystercatchers during my walk around. Several small groups of meadow pipits came in off the sea during the afternoon and also a single woodpigeon. A first-winter glaucous gull (presumably the same one as yesterday) arrived at the roost this evening, but the most striking bird of the day was a female merlin which I first saw chasing a pipit across the island, and later watched for about ten minutes perched on a rocky outcrop behind the engine room.

Merlins are great predators on open-country birds such as larks and pipits and so it is interesting that this one should arrive during a day of obvious pipit migration.

The strong westerly winds continue, now gusting up to gale force, but a few more waders were about this afternoon, although they fed on the seaward side of the island and kept to the more sheltered parts of the shore. A little flock of ten dunlin were new since yesterday and they fed·amongst a mixed flock of turnstones and purple sandpipers, showing a preference for the shallow pools. 'Our' glaucous gull was down on the foreshore from about midday and I saw it eating a large dead cod while several herring gulls kept a respectful distance.

Dead fish often turn up among the masses of weed thrown ashore, usually common species like codling or coley, occasionally a dogfish or conger eel. The weed forests offshore are the home of large numbers of fish, and lumpsuckers must be quite common, for I found several quite large ones amongst the weed. These are striking if not very attractive fish with rough, knobbly skin and no obvious scales. They are bottom living, and do not have a swim-bladder – the internal air reservoir most bony fish possess that gives them buoyancy. Their ventral fins are adapted to form a strong suction pad on their belly, just behind their head, which they use to anchor themselves onto the seabed during the flooding and ebbing of the tide. In Denmark 'Lumpfish Roe' is processed and sold as a type of caviar, but the fish is seldom eaten in Britain. I found a large male weighing about five pounds washed ashore, and made some drawings before I left it to the gulls.

A much rarer fish, which is quite new to me, is the Ray's bream, an aggressive looking deep-water creature with large teeth and an appearance rather reminiscent of some fossil fish I have seen. I found one today very dehydrated and partly eaten, above the high-water mark, and another washed up among some kelp (*Plate 5*). This too had been partly eaten but sufficient remained to make some sketches. It's a very mysterious fish, most of my reference books say nothing is known of its life cycle, other than that it is an inhabitant of the mid-Atlantic and small numbers are caught in the Mediterranean and off northern Norway. After I had drawn it, I left this one for the gulls too. Somehow I didn't feel like eating it!

While I was scratching around among the tideline debris this morning I found part of the skeleton of an eider, gleaming clean and white amongst a tangle of weed. Closer examination showed it to be ringed, the number

OYSTERCATCHER
Haematopus ostralegus
Coquet Island
adult ♀
4th January

winglength: 261 mm
bill length: 80mm
tarsus length: 51 mm

Found moribund on shore,
died ca. 90 minutes later.

(Plate 4)

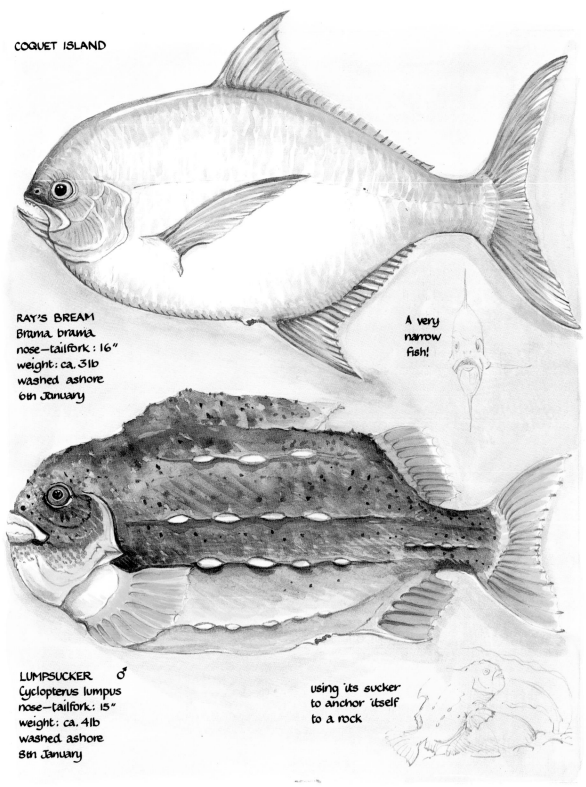

COQUET ISLAND

RAY'S BREAM
Brama brama
nose–tailfork: 16"
weight: ca. 3lb
washed ashore
6th January

A very
narrow
fish!

LUMPSUCKER ♂
Cyclopterus lumpus
nose–tailfork: 15"
weight: ca. 4lb
washed ashore
8th January

using its sucker
to anchor itself
to a rock

(Plate 5)

HW05471. By sending the ring to the British Trust for Ornithology I eventually learnt that the bird had been a breeding female ringed on Coquet on 30th May 1967 by research workers from Durham University.

Eiders are probably the most conspicuous birds around Coquet and a quick glance from any window on the lighthouse will show groups of ten or fifteen bobbing in the surf or lazing among the coarse grasses above the beach (*Plate 6*). I had not seen them either so close or in such numbers before, and spent quite a lot of my free time watching them.

Whenever the high tide floods in over the rocky shelf surrounding the island groups of drakes, with the occasional duck in attendance, drift in and start diving among the rocky pools and weed forests, bobbing buoyantly back to the surface with clusters of mussels or crabs in their bills. Where the water covering the pools is shallow enough they up-end to snatch shellfish from the crevices, and seem to find quite a lot of their food in a relatively small area. The feeding groups seem to ripple on the water as each bird dives just after the previous one, only to re-appear in almost the same place a few seconds later. At low tide the groups congregate much farther out, where the rock shelf ends and the water suddenly becomes ten to fifteen feet deeper. Here they feed in a less intense way, diving leisurely and often coming up several yards away, after which they swim back to re-join their group. There is a lot more squabbling, often a paired duck and drake in a dispute with an adjacent pair. They seldom actually come to blows, but there is much posturing and 'roo-kooing' from the drakes, and rather a lot of intense posturing and displaying by groups of males to a usually disinterested female. Many of the drakes are immature, showing a variety of blotchy-brown and white plumages, while some of the richly barred females seemed lighter in colour than others; this may also be a consequence of age.

Large numbers of eiders breed on Coquet during the summer and while I was wandering through the walled garden at the rear of the main building I found an old nest with five addled eggs in it. Obscured by dead nettles and other rank vegetation it was inconspicuous, and even after seven months the fine down was soft and dry. The eggs were rather discoloured and clammy, so I didn't handle them too much!

On the whole the eiders seemed confident about the presence of people. They are not persecuted on the north-east coast, and provided they can keep you in sight don't seem to mind an approach to within forty or fifty yards. One drake, dozing among the coarse vegetation above the beach, let me approach to within twenty yards before he got up and waddled off, a little pompously but without haste, to the tide's edge.

The eider is St Cuthbert's duck, pre-eminent among the seafowl to whom he preached his sermons during his long isolation on the Farne Islands. Quite what the ducks thought of his lessons history doesn't record, but after taking the time to watch them, and experiencing their tameness at first hand, it is plain to see why he found them so enchanting.

A low tide this morning gave me an opportunity to investigate the rock pools around the island, and also meant that larger numbers of waders and duck were apparent than previously. Little groups of purple sandpipers and turnstones were scattered over the whole shore and must have totalled fifty of each, while a quick count of the curlew suggested a similar figure, feeding in ones and twos among the weedy pools. Three goldeneye, a drake and two ducks, were diving off the northern tip of the island, and I had excellent views of a female red-breasted merganser diving for small fish in the boat landing *(Plate 7)*. At one stage she came right below the steps and I could see her swimming around under water, paddling with her feet, wings closed tight against her body.

The many rock pools in the sandstone reef around the island are very rich feeding grounds for birds at all stages of the tide. At high water they are covered to a depth of three to four feet, and large numbers of eider move in to dive for the abundant mussels. At low tide waders forage among the weed and pools, while gulls scavenge and steal from other birds.

In many ways the fauna of these pools is very different from the familiar one at home in Pembrokeshire. Fewer sea-anemones, but large numbers of big whelks, at this time of the year spawning their clusters of yellow, bubbly eggs in the deeper pools. The gulls are very keen on whelks, flying up and dropping them onto the rocks to shatter their shells and expose the vulnerable animal inside. The dominant seaweed is different too; the egg wrack is not uncommon in west Wales, but here forms huge mats which completely obscure the underlying rocks and in the more sheltered pools forms fronds three to four feet long. Familiar weeds such as bladder wrack and serrated wrack cling to the rocks in deeper crevices, hiding mussels far bigger and more purple than any at home. These are horse mussels, growing to over four inches in length alongside common mussels, which are big if they reach an inch and a half long. The eiders spend most of their feeding time diving over the most extensive mussel beds, but occasionally come up with a starfish or a crab. Green shore crabs are abundant, but in pools with sandy bottoms the dark-red velvet swimming crabs with their flattened, spade-like hind legs are common, moving quickly into new cover every time I pull away the sheltering weeds *(Plate 8)*.

Turning over rocks and weed reveals numbers of rather shy animals: slippery butterfish, rich brown with bold dark spots along their flanks; shrimps twitching nervous whiskers from the safety of a crevice; occasionally a small sea urchin. Among the most attractive creatures, quite new to me, are the hydroid sea firs, delicately branched fronds only a couple of inches high, which form miniature twiggy forests in the shallow pools. The tiny creatures which live in each segment filter micro-organisms from the sea water by means of minute feathery tentacles. The striking thing about them is the colour, all shades from pale yellow through orange to coral pinks, but this fades to a chalky white when they die.

EIDER STUDIES   Coquet Island, January

Group feeding in the tiderace.

← immature drake

Displaying group

(Plate 6)

SEA DUCKS
Coquet
January

imm. ♂

Common Scoter

Golden Eye

♀

♂ displaying

Redbreasted Merganser

♀

(Plate 7)

The dense seaweed mats hold vast numbers of sandhoppers, crabs and tiny fish, which attract waders in great numbers as the tide drops. Turnstones and purple sandpipers chivvy and bully each other through the weed, while sedate curlews stalk over the rocks, occasionally winkling out a large crab with their slender bills. The dropping tide sometimes strands quite large fish in the pools, codling or coley up to about a pound in weight, and that attracts gulls to squabble and fight over it until possession is finally resolved and the unfortunate fish is eaten.

JANUARY 10th   A small party of knot passed over the lighthouse this morning and when I went down to the beach after lunch fifteen were feeding together on the wet sand. Good numbers of purple sandpipers and turnstone were scattered over the shore, and I counted at least fifty curlew picking over the weed banks. Several unidentified divers had appeared offshore in the past few days and I finally got a good enough view of one to confirm it as a red-throated diver. This one dived with elegant fluidity in the clear water of the boat landing, and I got within thirty feet by playing 'grandmother's steps' and sneaking closer while the bird was under the surface. Once it noticed me, however, it dived quickly and re-appeared many seconds later about seventy yards offshore. This seems to be typical of divers in general, and I never got close to them other than by this deception.

An immature shag came ashore among the rocks below the tower, and although apparently uninjured, it died within ten minutes. A post-mortem during skinning gave no further clue to the cause of its death and I finished making up the study skin none the wiser.

JANUARY 11th   No birdwatching as such for we spent the day pumping fresh water to the header tanks and filling the oil store from the forty-gallon drums on the boat landing. This is a three-man job and, as the newcomer, I got the task of stacking the empty drums and lashing them down behind the store to await collection by the lighthouse tender. Most of the time I spent on this task I was overseen by a group of half a dozen eider, which sat on the rocks below the landing, making occasional sorties into the water to bathe and preen.

JANUARY 12th   A deterioration in the weather brought single knot and grey plover to the rock pools and a substantial concentration of purple sandpiper and

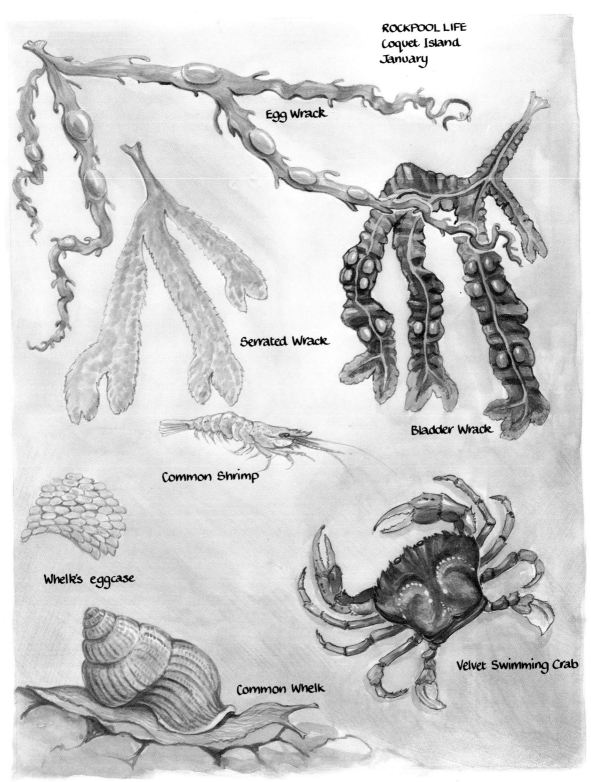

ROCKPOOL LIFE
Coquet Island
January

Egg Wrack

Serrated Wrack

Bladder Wrack

Common Shrimp

Whelk's eggcase

Common Whelk

Velvet Swimming Crab

(Plate 8)

turnstones. The strong winds, force five to seven, tended to keep the flocks feeding in sheltered spots, so I attempted a count of the numbers by starting at the boat landing and working right round the coastline, counting each group separately. It was difficult to know what to do about odd groups which 'leap-frogged' up the shore but I tried to avoid counting them twice, and arrived at figures of 109 purple sandpipers and 87 turnstones. I picked up a freshly dead adult great black-backed gull this evening and added a drawing of it to the immature I found the other day before making it up as a study skin (*Plate 9*).

JANUARY 13th   Just after 6.00 a.m. this morning, while I was emptying the rubbish bins, I heard a small group of skylarks passing over the lighthouse, coming from the north-east. It was still quite dark, the weather squally with showers, wind southerly force six to seven. As it got light other small groups of skylarks came in off the sea, passing over Coquet and on to the mainland opposite. The little flocks came in steadily at much the same height from the east and north-east, and arrived early to mid-morning after a flight which probably started on the Scandinavian coast the previous night, about 400 miles away. The mortality on these night crossings must be immense and the hazards do not end with an arrival on the English shore, for this morning one group of three or four skylarks was met by a female merlin, seemingly intent on an exhausted skylark for an easy meal. She launched her attack on one individual as it came over the island and repeatedly spiralled above it and made short dives onto it. This particular skylark proved more than a match for her, however, and managed to climb up above the merlin time and again until after three or four minutes the small falcon gave up and took to her perch on the rocky outcrop beyond the lighthouse wall. Later on in the day I visited her chosen vantage point, and found the wings and legs of a freshly-killed redshank, which had been less able to evade her than the larks. Over the past few days I have found several fresh remains of shore waders, and although I haven't seen the merlin every day, I am sure she has been using the island as a regular feeding place.

   The first-winter glaucous gull has been spending the whole day around the island lately and today I saw it catch a dunlin, which appeared to be ailing, kill it with two or three hammer blows from its great beak and swallow it whole!

JANUARY 14th   Today should have been my relief day, but I am staying on for a further turn of duty as one of the keepers due to come on station has reported sick.

GREAT BLACK-BACKED GULL
Larus marinus
Coquet Island

full wingspan: ca. 60"
wing length: 502 mm
bill length: 66 mm

adult ♂
found dead at roost
12th January

1st-winter bird
found dead at roost
3rd January

winglength: 480 mm
bill length: 60 mm

outer
tailfeather,
1st-winter

(Plate 9)

Geordie and Jack left, however, to be replaced by Fred, Principal Keeper, and Paul. The day was largely taken up with the normal relief chores, but while we were waiting on the boat landing I saw our first-winter glaucous gull, and a short while later a much paler second-winter bird. Towards dusk both were in the gull roost together, much to the consternation of the smaller gulls.

JANUARY 16th   After the squally and showery weather recently today was calmer with light southerly winds. This change seemed to affect the small passerine birds, for the island wrens were joined by a pair of blackbirds and later on a pair of goldfinches. There was also a steady passage of skylarks this morning, and the calmer weather gave me an opportunity to go through the waders more carefully than recently. Purple sandpiper numbers continue to increase with a single flock today containing in excess of 90 birds, while the island as a whole held over 120. Turnstone numbers were much as previously, about 60 feeding in scattered groups, joined on the sandiest part of the shore by single knot and ringed plover. Curlew numbers were higher than they have been for a while, and when the high tide came a flock of 47 congregated near the boat landing, although my impression during the day was of rather more than that about the island.

Apart from the gulls and eiders, the most obvious birds around Coquet are the waders of the rocky shore. Although they all live together on the inter-tidal zone, they exploit the habitat in subtly different ways, which often betray the character of the species. Turnstone, for example, feed busily over the whole shoreline, and in bad weather come inland to poke among the rabbit burrows and low walls around the lighthouse garden. At low tide they argue and squabble among the seaweed beds, chasing shrimps and small shellfish, occasionally catching tiny crabs. When the tide is high they move up to the debris zone at the top of the beach and turn over dead seaweed, bits of wood and other rubbish, seeking sandhoppers.  Sometimes two or three birds co-operate to turn a large piece of weed but they are just as likely to be working against each other from opposite sides, each trying to tip it onto the other. Dead fish or bird corpses on the shore also attract turnstones, and I've seen them snapping up scraps of flesh scattered by the squabbling of large gulls, just like jackals around feeding lions! They are sociable birds, often feeding inter-mixed with other shore waders such as dunlin, redshanks and purple sandpipers. Above all they are perpetually busy, feeding constantly and transferring their attentions above the shore when the flooding tide forces all other species into uneasy rest.

Purple sandpipers, on the other hand, are less obtrusive, feeding quietly along the rocks, picking among the crevices and weed. Breeding as they do on the tundra of northern Norway and Iceland they seldom meet people, and as a consequence are tame and trusting to the point where they will jostle sedately to pick up scraps of fish thrown to them from only four or five feet away. Coquet in January is exceptionally good for them, several groups of fifteen or twenty feed above the island, and occasionally a high-tide roost will bring 70 to 80 birds together on the rocks by the boat landing, providing superb views of these dapper, gentle, soft-grey birds so well adapted to their rather bleak winter home.

Redshanks, curlew and oystercatchers are also regular feeders on the shore, but their numbers seem much more variable and movements between the island and the nearby coast are regular and often involve good numbers of birds coming into the island to feed at low tide. Oystercatchers descend on the mussel beds in noisy piebald flocks, while scattered curlew, finding it difficult to probe the rocks with their slender bills, pull protesting crabs from the weedy pools. Redshanks are their characteristically noisy selves, flying up to mob intruders quite fearlessly, behaviour which gives other shorebirds warning of the approach of predators, which is just as well when, as now, a female merlin moves in to take over the island for a couple of weeks. She hunts the shore waders mercilessly, killing at least one a day, mostly turnstones and redshanks, but occasionally a purple sandpiper or dunlin. She leaves the wings and legs of her victims lying below the two or three rocky promontories she uses as plucking posts, and these provide an insight into the origins of some of the redshanks. When I collect the wings and take careful measurements, two or three individuals show a wing length in excess of 170 mm, indicating that they probably belong to the larger Icelandic race. British and European redshanks have shorter wings which seem to me to be browner and less grey, although this is not apparent when they are on the shore.

High tide and rough weather occasionally brings other species of waders to the island, particularly species more often associated with the long sandy beaches and mud flats of the adjacent coast. Ringed plover are common on the rocky coats of west Wales, but only occasionally turn up on Coquet, picking around among the rough grass and tideline rubbish along the short sandy beach. They are much more common on the mainland and many pairs must breed in the miles of sand-dune coast around Bamburgh and Holy Island.

Grey plover sometimes appear, to pick around the weedy fringes of the pools for small invertebrates. They are gentle birds, with a perpetual 'worried' expression, and avoid the squabblings of more argumentative species like oystercatchers and turnstones by keeping discreetly to the fringes of feeding flocks. Their wolf-whistling calls and distinctive black 'armpits' make them easy to locate and identify as they pass by offshore and most of the birds I see are drifting north, probably making for the Lindisfarne Reserve.

JANUARY 19th   The settling of the weather over the past few days has resulted in a decline in the numbers of shore waders, and I could only find half a dozen redshank and about forty purple sandpipers this morning. There seemed to be rather more fulmars around than previously, and several pairs were in occupation of ledges and indulging in throaty, chortling displays.

A single red-throated diver passed by offshore during the morning, being carried northwards on the flooding tide. It showed signs of oil staining on its flanks and upper breast.

JANUARY 21st   Much colder and rather more blustery, the forecast indicating sleet and snow-showers. I woke up this morning to find a robin in the lighthouse garden, feeding on some of the scraps we left out the previous days. Wader numbers remain low, but a first-winter glaucous gull was around again this afternoon, and I watched it steal the carcase of a rabbit from a group of first-winter herring gulls.

Despite the cold and blustery conditions two wrens were feeding among the rocks above the debris zone. They avoided the chilling wind by feeding in the deep cavities under the bigger boulders where there seemed to be a good supply of invertebrates. In all probability the deep accumulations of rotting seaweed nearby meant that many insects which feed on the shore debris in summer and autumn over-winter in these deep but sheltered recesses.

The event of the day was the arrival of a large bird, seen diving in the boat landing this morning. I couldn't make much of it at first, but when I moved around the little bay and got the sun behind me I saw it was an immature great northern diver, which obligingly stayed most of the afternoon. It dived repeatedly, often staying submerged for a minute or more, but I never saw it surface with a fish. Unlike shags and cormorants, which invariably bring their catches to the surface, divers seem to either swallow their fish underwater, or they are worse fishermen than I had supposed.

JANUARY 22nd–23rd   Heavy rain early in the morning of the 22nd turned to persistent drizzle by midday, with steadily increasing winds which reached southerly gale force by late evening. It grew colder towards dusk and eventually sleet and then heavier snow developed, bringing a full-scale blizzard by about midnight. I was on middle watch, and spent most of my four hours up in the lantern dressed in waterproofs and armed with a broom, making frequent sorties onto the gallery to clear the snow off the lantern glazing. The wind was still force eight and gusting a little bit more, and I could see the great wet snow-flakes coming horizontally out of the blackness all around. They hit the glazing with the impact of a snowball and stuck there! In only a few minutes the panes of glass were thick with snow significantly obscuring the light, hence my virgil in the lantern, where despite the cold I was sweating in waterproofs! Fortunately, the worst of the blizzard only lasted a couple of hours, so after about 2 a.m. I was able to go down for a cup of tea. By the end of my watch the snow had turned to hard stinging sleet and when I got up mid-morning on the 23rd the snow had all disappeared. Not so the wind, however, for the gale increased through the morning, reaching south-west force nine, gusting ten by midday. The sun came out in the afternoon, and visibility increased markedly, but by nightfall it started to rain heavily again. Weather like this seriously curtails birdwatching, but did give me a chance to do some drawing and also catch up on reading. Surprisingly enough in the midst of that foul weather we were visited by a flock of nine goldfinches which fed in the shelter of the garden wall for most of the two days.

An improvement in the weather, still squally but only about force five, brought back the purple sandpipers with a vengeance. In a single flock below the landing I counted more than eighty, all methodically picking over the weedy rocks, while the island held probably a hundred or more. Turnstones were up to their former levels, and I found a couple of dunlin feeding in one of the larger rock pools. There was a winter plumage guillemot offshore and just after midday a flock of seven divers flew north, but too far out to identify specifically. Around the garden the local wrens were joined by a robin and a song thrush, which may well have been present right through the storm but keeping a low profile, sheltering among the rocky walls.

JANUARY 24th

Not surprisingly the beach and shoreline was a mass of seaweed and debris. Several fish boxes had come ashore, some still intact and bearing the names of Scottish fishing villages such as Pittenweem and Anstruther, and bits of netting and other timber, masses of whelk shells and lightbulbs, miraculously unbroken, unwholesome looking grapefruit and a pomegranate. Feathers and dead fish, lead weights and fishing tackle caught up among bladder wrack, a wellington boot, a frogman's flipper and a sandal – and much more besides.

Apart from the endless plastic bottles and cans, many of them foreign in origin, strange objects turn up which can take quite a bit of identifying. This morning I found two huge yellow feet, obviously from a bird, but rather thick with tough scales and strong claws. They had been hacked off and were rather sinister-looking. Only the close association of the second one with a derelict Christmas tree persuaded me that they were turkey feet, discarded in the aftermath of an ocean-going Christmas dinner!

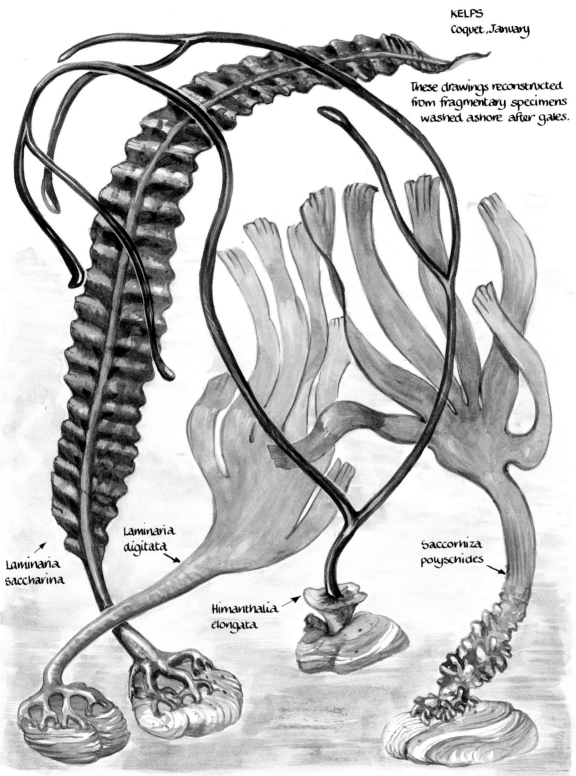

KELPS
Coquet, January

These drawings reconstructed
from fragmentary specimens
washed ashore after gales.

Laminaria
digitata

Laminaria
saccharina

Saccorhiza
polyschides

Himanthalia
elongata

(Plate 10)

All these other treasures have to be sorted out from the great rolled-up masses of seaweed, torn from the dense forests below the low-water mark. Most people refer to the tough, brown, leathery weeds as kelp, although this name is properly reserved for only a few of the world's species. It's not wildly attractive stuff, but is quite useful and in many parts of the world it is harvested for fertiliser. Agar jelly is extracted from it, to be used in laboratories for growing cultures and bacteria. Most of the specimens washed ashore are broken fragments, but I did collect four different species to make some drawings for future reference (*Plate 10*).

JANUARY 25th

Both 'my' glaucous gulls were around today, feeding on different parts of the shore. The second-winter bird seems more confident and self-assured than the first-winter, and dominates all the other gulls it feeds with. They both share a preference for carrion, either fish, bird or rabbit, and I haven't seen them searching for crabs and shellfish like the smaller gulls.

A number of kittiwakes were feeding off the north end for most of the afternoon, but their comings and goings made it difficult to count them, I imagine there to have been twenty to thirty, a good number of them in immature plumage. The roost was joined by a group of eleven common gulls, which arrived just before dusk, and settled on a rocky outcrop away from the larger gulls. Small numbers pass by on most days, but these are the first I have seen coming into the roost. Our trio of divers is complete, for the boat landing held a black-throated diver this morning. It wasn't diving much and moved on northwards only a few minutes after I had set up my telescope.

JANUARY 28th

The past few days have seen a recurrence of the bad weather, with visibility very poor due to drizzle and sleet, and steadily increasing winds reaching gale force today. We sounded the fog signal yesterday for a time but the strengthening wind seems to have improved things a little by blowing the mist away. Birds have been very thin on the ground, although the second-winter glaucous gull turned up yesterday, so I turned my attention to rabbits which are present on Coquet in very large numbers.

The island is very closely cropped at this time of the year, and many of the rabbits feed on the seashore nibbling seaweed from the rocks. One or two very emaciated corpses I had found had their stomachs packed with chewed-up seaweed and winter mortality seems very high. I have found several gnawed whelk shells among the warrens and watched one big rabbit chewing on the wing bones of a gull's skeleton, all of which suggests they are lacking calcium in their diet. Every evening we would put all our vegetable peelings and other scraps out on the lawn in front of the living room window and sit inside to watch the rabbits coming in through the open gates of the walled garden to eat them. I couldn't be sure how many actually made use of these hand-outs, but usually ten to fifteen were in the garden at once, and sometimes over twenty showed up. One evening, when they were all feeding avidly, the other two keepers and I crept out of the back door and shut the garden gates on them, blocking the bottom of the gate with old bits of fishing net scavenged from the shore. In the next ten minutes we caught eleven, and the chance for a close examination showed them to be extremely thin but otherwise healthy. We let them all go unharmed and only half an hour later a good number were back in the garden for the extra large pile of scraps we had put out.

JANUARY 29th   The purple sandpiper flock below the landing has grown yet again. This morning I was watching them from the tower, and managed to count 154, feeding among the exposed rocks. We were rather busy with oil and water-pumping today so I only had the briefest look around but there must have been another 30 to 40 purple sandpipers at the other end of the island.

FEBRUARY 1st   A quiet and unimpressive day, with warm sun, no wind and very little in the way of birds. It became rather overcast this evening, and when I went to check on the light at 8.20 p.m. I found a small bird fluttering at the lantern glazing. I caught it, a fine male chaffinch, with beautifully rich pink underparts and a dark slaty head. I ringed it, number JV32827, and kept it in a cloth bag overnight because birds released while it is still dark and the light on remain disorientated.

FEBRUARY 2nd   The chaffinch flew off strongly towards the mainland this morning but apart from two goldfinches there was no sign of any other migrants. The sea was very calm, like the proverbial mill pond, and many of the drake eiders offshore were displaying vigorously, although the females seemed pretty disinterested. Three grey plover flew past southwards mid-morning, 'wolf-whistling' and flashing their black armpits.

FEBRUARY 3rd   Overcast and mild most of the day, but towards dusk sea fog came in rapidly and stayed through the night. A day remarkable for the numbers of

passerines around, which strongly suggested a significant passage over-night. A flock of thirty starlings were feeding avidly on the short turf outside the living room window, while the back garden held a robin and a pair of blackbirds. There were three or four song thrushes about and a flock of seven goldfinches picking over the rubbish dump. Out on the island itself half a dozen skylarks, and about the same number of meadow pipits, were feeding along the tideline. At 2.10 p.m. a single lapwing passed low over the island, making steadily towards the mainland.

FEBURARY 4th

Yesterday's migrants seem to have all gone, with the exception of a couple of song thrushes. A single fieldfare stopped briefly in the garden before flying on to the mainland this afternoon, otherwise it was a quiet day.

FEBRUARY 5th

After five weeks on Coquet, my relief arrived and I left the island by local boat at 11.15 a.m. It had been a good introduction to lightkeeping, with a Victorian oil burner and lots of seabirds and waders, and I genuinely felt sorry to leave, although the prospect of a week's home leave sweetened the moment.

The short crossing was soon over and a group of a hundred eider feeding in Amble Harbour, with a first-winter glaucous gull drifting casually over the river mouth, welcomed me back to the mainland again.

ST MARY'S ISLAND, NORTHUMBERLAND
55° 05′N; 1° 25′W

(Plate 11)

ST MARY'S ISLAND

The lighthouse on St Mary's Island dominates the view northwards across Whitley Bay, although the island itself is low and rocky, attached to the mainland by a half-mile long causeway which is covered by the sea at high tide (*Plate 11*). Adjacent to the lighthouse buildings is another low house which was formerly a tavern much frequented by smugglers, until the lighthouse was built in 1898. Men working on the foundations uncovered several stone coffins and skeletons from what was formerly the burial ground for the monks of Tynemouth Priory. Today the island attracts many visitors from the popular holiday resort of Whitley Bay and some of them are keen to look over the lighthouse. Very few people realise how important this low, rocky outcrop has been through the ages to a strange assortment of people.

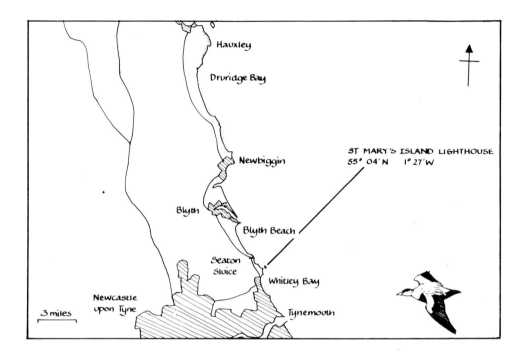

The station is normally manned by only two keepers, but at this time of the year the long nights require an additional man to share the workload and I was only one of a succession of junior keepers sent for three or four weeks at a stretch. Like Coquet, St Mary's is an oil-burning light but it differs in having a revolving lens driven by a big clockwork motor, which needs re-winding every fifty minutes. The lens is huge, constructed of bronze and heavy glass prisms and weighs all of four and a half tons. It floats in a bath of mercury, and this enables it to be driven by the clockwork motor, as the push of a single finger will set it revolving silently on its frictionless silver bed.

The close proximity of Whitley Bay means the convenience of fresh bread, meat and groceries, and the luxury of having milk delivered, at least as far as the mainland end of the causeway. Collecting the milk and the post is a job for the morning watchman, tides permitting.

Day trippers and holiday makers swarm over the rocks on bright sunny days, even at this time of the year, and it seems to me that many of them are unable to grasp the principles of the tide tables posted in the car park on the mainland opposite. A mid-afternoon high tide on a bright weekend will invariably trap a few on the rocks, and they are then faced with a three- or four-hour wait before the causeway is uncovered again. Most people take it in good humour, although some seem to imply that it is the lightkeeper's job to warn them, even though there are sufficient notices at both ends of the causeway.

The coastline north from St Mary's, although quite densely populated, is exceptionally good for birds, with many sites easily accessible by public transport. Fortunately, this is the local patch of a good bird-watching friend, George Miller, and he was able to show me many places which I might have otherwise overlooked.

I arrived at the lighthouse just after 10.00 a.m., a little bemused by taking a taxi right up to the front door! Les, the Principal Keeper, and Jim, his assistant, took me on a tour of the station and both seemed a little relieved that I knew a bit about oil lights. It seems that many of the junior keepers had no experience of them and consequently needed some nursing in their first few days. The tower is a pretty awe-inspiring feature, 120 feet high, with an open spiral staircase around the wall inside. It takes a good ten minutes at a steady pace to climb to the service room, just below the lantern, and I dread to think what it will be like washing down the steps with a mop and bucket!

FEBRUARY 15th

By mid-afternoon I had seen all there was to see and, after unpacking my gear, went out for a look around the island. It didn't seem terribly promising, bare and rocky, about a hundred yards long by fifty wide, and nowhere more than fifteen feet above sea-level. The only cover available for migrants were a few sorry-looking shrubs in the corner of the lighthouse garden, and even these didn't grow above the protection of the wall. I found out later that the soil they grew in had been brought over from the mainland some years previously! Seaweed fringed the whole island, and at low-water extensive rockpools and mussel beds were exposed, rather like those on Coquet Island.

The tide had covered the causeway and was steadily filling the main channel to the north-west of the island. I could see the current carrying odd clumps of weed and other debris around in a sweeping curve, eventually bringing it ashore below the cliff opposite. Quite suddenly a bird surfaced in the muddy water about fifty yards away and before I got my binoculars on it, dived again. When it re-appeared it was holding a franticly wriggling eel in its bill, and my binoculars showed it to be an extremely dapper-looking drake red-breasted merganser. While I was watching this, and also a female goldeneye which came drifting around the corner on the flooding tide, I began to see groups of waders coming on to the island from several directions, and realised that they were massing for a high-tide roost on the rocks behind the lighthouse (*Plate 12*). By great good fortune these rocks are over-looked by the living-room window of my quarters, so I went back inside, put the kettle on and set up my telescope to await developments.

After the experience of rock-shore waders on Coquet, it was interesting to see the effects of the long, sandy beaches to the north and south of the lighthouse. Far and away the most numerous birds were knot, and a very rough count indicated about 350 individuals, along with over 150 sanderlings. Both these species, associated with sandy beaches, were much less common on Coquet. Turnstone, ringed plover and purple sandpiper all mustered in the order of fifty birds and there were also small numbers of dunlin and curlew. Most of these birds were packed in a dense flock just above the high water mark and because of that were difficult to count accurately. Oystercatchers, however, arrived steadily in noisy groups of five and ten enabling me to count them with more confidence, arriving at a total of at least 132.

Very noticeable was the way that the flock quietened down towards high tide, with many of the birds dozing on one leg, and how quickly after the turn of the tide that some groups started leaving, as if they knew that by the time they reached their destination feeding grounds would be sufficiently exposed. Particularly noticeable in this respect were the sanderling, who seemed to arrive last and leave first on most occasions.

FEBRUARY 16th

Overcast and squally, with drizzle and low visibility. I walked over the causeway this morning to look at the shoreline opposite. Despite keeping a careful eye open I saw nothing exceptional in the bird line, other than a little flock of goldeneye, nine in all, with three very smart drakes displaying vigorously. Their striking black and white plumage was much enhanced by the strange contortions they adopt, but on this occasion it seemed to make little difference to the females, who remained aloof and uninterested.

With the shortage of birds, I turned my attention to the geology of the cliffs and a closer examination confirmed my impression that they are composed of different rock to the island and its adjacent promontory. These latter are a rough grainy sandstone, but on either side lie more horizontally bedded layers of shale, which being softer, are eroded much more quickly. I split some of the layered rock, and found numerous small fossils of branched creatures which go by the family name of graptolites, although I could not easily identify the species involved. These animals were widespread when the shales were laid down as mud under shallow seas and evolved into very many different forms, but they are all now extinct, leaving only their fossils behind.

In a couple of places seams of soft brown coal outcrop in the beds of shale, and these contained numerous fragmentary plant remains. In the past many people collected this 'sea-coal' for domestic use, but fewer do so today, although I did see a couple of men loaded down with dripping sackfuls.

HIGH TIDE ROOST
St Mary's Island
Compiled from sketches
made through telescope.

Immature Knot

Adult Knot

Ringed Plover

Adult

Immature

Sanderling

(Plate 12)

RINGED PLOVER AND DUNLIN
St Mary's Island Lighthouse
February

Birds at the roost on the rocks,
drawn from my living-room window
through a telescope.

The dunlin were feeding in the pools
on the splash zone as the tide fell.

Note the centre of gravity of a sleeping bird.

(Plate 13)

George and his friend Peter came over to the lighthouse this morning, and after a brief walk along the beach, during which we found an oiled guillemot, we settled down to watch the waders coming in to roost and lay some plans to visit other sites nearby. The roost produced much the same number of birds as previously, but we did see a nice first-winter glaucous gull on the tideline and a rather unexpected grey wagtail feeding around the rockpools on the causeway (*Plate 13*). Eventually it flew off towards the mainland, leaving us a little puzzled as to its purpose, so far from the freshwater streams which form its usual habitat.

FEBRUARY 17th

With only a couple of hours around midday to spare, I followed a suggestion made by George yesterday and walked along the top of the cliffs whose fossils I had examined the other day. This brought me out about a mile up the coast at Seaton sluice, where the Seaton burn runs into the sea. Here, according to my local expert, there should be some seaduck. Sure enough a flock of piebald bodies in the broken water just offshore proved to be about fifteen eider, and in a short while I noticed a long line of dark brown or sooty black ducks a bit farther out. These were easily identified as common scoter, but it took me a while to count them, as they were seldom all on the surface at the same time. I ended up with a figure of twenty or so, but before the count was complete four more ducks joined the flock, and closer examination revealed them as goldeneye. From my vantage point on the cliff top it was easy to sort them out as an adult drake, a rather more blotchy immature drake, and two females. Only the gentlest of breezes came in from the south-west, but a bit of a swell from offshore added to the surge of water from the Seaton burn meant that all these ducks were riding a constant roller-coaster, being lifted high on the crests and disappearing into the troughs. Add to this their regular diving for food and it is easy to see why I wandered back to St Mary's a little unsure of my figures.

FEBRUARY 18th

Working around the lighthouse all day, the morning view was rather limited by fog. By mid-morning it had cleared a little, but the rocks were pretty empty of birds except for a summer-plumage guillemot just offshore and an immature shag, which was wearing a metal ring on one leg (*Plate 15*). Both these birds showed signs of oiling and I have noticed a few of the gulls along the beach with the filthy brown stuff smeared on their feathers.

FEBRUARY 19th

This was my first day free of duty, so I met George at the bus stop outside Whitley Bay cemetery, where we caught a bus to Blyth South Harbour.

FEBRUARY 20th

COD AND FIVEBEARDED ROCKLING
St Mary's Island
February

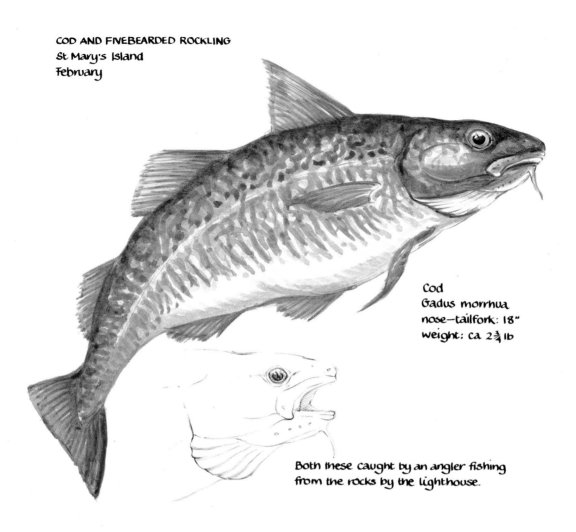

Cod
Gadus morrhua
nose—tailfork: 18"
weight: ca 2¾ lb

Both these caught by an angler fishing
from the rocks by the lighthouse.

Fivebearded Rockling
Ciliata mustela
nose—tail tip: 10"
weight: ca 10 oz

(Plate 14)

Among the gulls around the piers we found a second-winter glaucous gull, but the two-mile walk back along Blyth beach to Seaton sluice produced little more than a rotten Ray's bream, a couple of goldeneye and a lot of drizzle. We arrived at the pub overlooking Seaton sluice in time for a pint and some toasted sandwiches, after which we went out to look at the sea, and by a joint effort succeeded in counting the common scoter, making their number to be twenty-one. Exhausted by this feat of ornithological mathematics and unimpressed by the drizzle, we went back into the pub for more brown ale and toasted sandwiches, until the licensing laws compelled us to leave.

Having tired of the salt sea spray, we turned inland and followed the Seaton burn through Hollywelldene, where we found a grey wagtail feeding in its proper habitat along the fast-flowing brook, and eventually arrived in late afternoon at Hollywell ponds, where we settled down in what little shelter we could find, to have a look at the ducks gathered on the water. The most obvious inhabitants were a large herd of whooper swans, thirty-one in total. These were feeding in the shallows at the far side of the pond, and totally ignored three immature mute swans which loitered nearby. More than half of the whoopers were immature, although I didn't actually count them, and several of the adults showed a deep orange colour on their heads, caused by iron-staining in the waters on their breeding grounds. A good number of dabbling duck were feeding in the shallows around the swans, probably a hundred mallard, with more arriving every couple of minutes, thirty wigeon and about twenty teal. I kept getting a brief glimpse of a pale breast among the scrum of ducks in the shallows, but it took some time before this resolved itself as a fine drake pintail in full breeding plumage, complete with long tail.

I could have spent the rest of our time there watching the ducks jostling in the weedy pools, but we moved on to the opposite end of the lake, where the deeper water held a flock of diving ducks, all of whom seemed to be sleeping at first glance, although a careful scrutiny showed that many apparently sleeping birds had a watchful eye cast in our direction. These seemed to be predominantly tufted duck, but we did pick out three chestnut-headed pochard drakes and about ten female or immature goldeneye. By now the drizzle had turned to rain and dusk gathered ever closer, so we called it a day, and headed back towards St Mary's flushing a very indignant short-eared owl on the way.

Early morning fog, giving way to a sunny and mild day. I set out to walk into Whitley Bay to do some shopping and was pleased to find a short-eared owl quartering the fields just beyond the mainland end of the causeway. Although they are daytime hunters short-eareds are rather shy of people, and I was lucky to get some excellent views of it beating slowly back and forth over the rough grass and eventually perching on a fence post near the roadway, plainly visible in the bright sunlight.

When my shopping was completed I walked back along the tideline, looking for dead birds. Almost any stretch of beach will produce the remains of seabirds, many the victims of oil pollution. Those that dive for their food – auks, cormorants, divers and grebes – are most badly affected, but many of the gulls which scavenge on the shoreline have oil patches on their plumage. This morning's walk produced a couple of badly oiled guillemots and an immature shag, which was in fairly good condition. This I decided to bring back to the lighthouse, to make a few reference drawings, as it was only very slightly oil damaged, unlike most of the other birds I find (*Plate 15*).

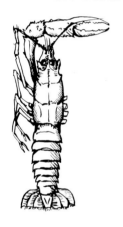

FEBRUARY 23rd   George and I spent the morning at North Shields Fish Quay, patiently searching through the endless gull flocks for any sign of the rarer species which sometimes occur there. Alas, all the gulls were our familiar British species. It was a bit strange to see kittiwakes perching on the roof-tops, but they nest on the riverside warehouses further up the river, so on the Tyne they are probably more blasé about perching on man-made structures than those from the west coast sea cliffs at home. I was very surprised to see a grey seal swimming between the fishing boats moored along the quay, and as we walked along it followed us expectantly, until it swam past a boat where two men were gutting fish. One of them looked up and said: 'Oh aye, yon seal,' picked up a couple of small codling and a handful of fishguts and threw them into the water. This was obviously what the seal expected us to do for it ate its free fish quickly before moving on along the moorings. It seems, from what the fishermen told us, that this particular seal seldom went far from the quay and made a good living from the kindness of the boat crews.

Rare gulls being notable by their absence, we bought a couple of pounds of Dublin Bay Prawns (known as Norway Lobsters up here and sold in the shops, after processing, as scampi) took them back to St Mary's Island and sat on the rocks behind the lighthouse watching waders and eating prawns.

FEBRUARY 24th   Very dense fog through the night and persisting all day, visibility no more than half a mile. I was on morning watch, and at 6.00 a.m. went up to the lantern to check on the weather and found a song thrush fluttering at the glazing. I caught it, and finding it to be uninjured ringed it, number XA84401. I let it go at daybreak, just after 7.30 a.m., and it flew away strongly towards the mainland.

About an hour later I went across to collect the post and milk and found a heron fishing in the rock pools along the causeway. It flew a short distance to one side as I passed, but quickly returned and stayed fishing there until about half past nine, when a couple walking a dog put it up and it flew off westwards.

Today produced a surprise, but I suspect that I was the only person caught unawares. George, Peter and I spent the lunchtime playing darts in a pub at Wallsend, then we wandered off to look at the Swallow Marsh, a series of shallow pools caused by colliery subsidence, close to George's home. We soon found a good number of mallard and tufted duck, and a very tame pair of whooper swans. The female apparently met with an accident involving overhead cables a few years previously, and when she flapped her wings it was plain to see that half of her left wing was completely gone. The male stayed with her and in the spring, when the other whoopers were leaving, he remained behind with his incapacitated mate, and has been here ever since. The surprise came to me when we reached the other end of the marsh, for standing in the shallows was a very tall, rather pink, Chilean flamingo (*Plate 16*)! George finally admitted that it had been in the area for some months but still claimed he didn't know it would be there for certain. It surprised me that it could find sufficient food and it seemed fit and healthy in spite of the sleet and drizzle which developed towards dusk. Some birdwatchers would dismiss it as 'only an escape', but surely that misses the point of it? On a cold grey day, such a striking and elegantly beautiful bird is undoubtedly a bonus to be grateful for.

FEBRUARY 26th

Another foggy start to the day, but it quickly brightened up into a sunny if rather cold afternoon. The heron was back among the rockpools again this morning, but a short distance from the causeway, so my trip across for the milk didn't disturb him. When I was collecting the milk I saw first one, and then a second short-eared owl hunting over the rough grass behind the car park.

FEBRUARY 27th

When I finished my various chores I took a walk over the rocks to the area used by the wader roost, to have a closer look at something lying in a pool, which I had seen from up on the gallery. It turned out to be a dead knot, in immaculate condition and with no apparent sign of injury. The pupil of its right eye was completely milky-white, however, and I imagine it must have been blind in that eye.

When the tide came in this afternoon I had another good look at the wader flocks, and noted that although the knot numbers seemed pretty

SHAG
Phalacrocorax aristotelis
immature
washed ashore oiled
Whitley Bay Beach
21st February

This drawing made
after the oil had been
cleaned off its breast
and wing with soap.

winglength: 262 mm
bill length: 57mm

(Plate 15)

FLAMINGO
Swallow Marsh
Wallsend
26th February
South American subspecies
Phoenicopterus ruber chilensis

Noticeably white through lack of correct diet, but otherwise very healthy.

(Plate 16)

stable, there was a substantial increase in the purple sandpipers with close on 200 packed in a tight group just above the tideline.

FEBRUARY 28th   The early morning fog didn't clear today, but persisted as a moderate sea-mist. My trip across the causeway to fetch the milk was heronless, but one of the short-eared owls was quartering the rough field methodically and while I was watching it dropped into the ditch, presumably on a small rodent, and did not reappear. Walking back to the lighthouse, I noticed that a small fish in one of the shallow pools much frequented by our absent heron. It took some catching but was clearly a gunnel (*Pholis gunnellus*), in a very attractive light red-brown phase with yellow fins, that I had not seen previously. Also known as butterfish in some parts of Britain because they are incredibly slippery, this one proved it by disappearing through my fingers into a very weedy pool.

George came up to the lighthouse in the afternoon, bringing something special from Blyth Beach. In the course of his walk he had found several oiled razorbills and guillemots, but from his bag he produced an oiled little auk! This is the first one I have seen, quite literally 'in the flesh', and although it had been dead a few days I made some study drawings before skinning it (*Plate 17*). This bird is a high Arctic breeder which is particularly numerous in Greenland and Spitzbergen. Single colonies have been estimated to contain over a million birds and the local people in Greenland still net large numbers for food. It is only rarely washed ashore, and is even less frequently seen alive in Britain, but 'wrecks' (large numbers of auks appearing inland after severe storms) do occur from time to time during autumn gales, when exhausted individuals turn up often miles inland. They are specialist feeders, primarily hunting macro-plankton, and consequently they are very difficult to rehabilitate in captivity. George has found quite a number on the north-east coast over the years and has given me several skins, but it was very nice to be able to examine the structure of this little bird at first hand. One of the most striking features was a number of hard bony projections from the roof of its mouth which presumably assist it in swallowing its prey.

MARCH 1st   On my last free day, George and Peter took me on an extended tour of some of the very best stretches of the Northumbrian coast. We started from Fenham Low Moor, the southern shore of the Lindisfarne National Nature Reserve and walked around the coast to the navigation pinnacles on the point opposite Holy Island. It was low tide, so we saw rather few birds, but the vast sweep of mud flats running north and east to the low mass of Holy

Island itself provided a tremendous backdrop to the scattered flocks of curlew, shelduck and bar-tailed godwits feeding out on the mud (*Plate 18*). From the pinnacles we turned south along Skate Road, a seemingly endless beach which must be four miles long and unbroken by anything man-made. It faces the open sea and so we started to find dead birds, mostly oiled gulls and the odd dead guillemot, but a few rotten eiders and a long-dead red-throated diver. Most surprising were two puffins, one still in the dull winter plumage and another complete with bright bill in full breeding plumage. I kept them both for reference, as they were not oiled but very emaciated. After our walk down the Skate Road and through the sand dunes, George's father picked us up and we went by car around to Budle Bay, where we ate our lunch overlooking a large mixed flock of duck feeding on the estuary. From the comfort of a car, with tea and sandwiches, it should have been easy enough to count them, but we couldn't agree on a figure and ended up with an estimated 150 wigeon and 30 each of shelduck and teal. Our last stop on the way home was Bamburgh, as much to see the quite incredible castle as to birdwatch. The whole beach is overshadowed by the massive outcrop of rock on which the castle is built and from the shoreline careful attention to detail means that nothing of the twentieth century can be seen and it is easy to imagine what the area must have been like during the particularly violent past the north-east coast has seen.

The day was not quite done when we found a dead female grey seal on the beach. It was quite fresh and George and I, both having worked as taxidermists before, rose to the task of skinning it armed with nothing more than two pen-knives. It took us over an hour, during which Peter dug a big hole in the sand to bury the carcase. We were all very pleased with the success of the operation, even though George's father insisted we smelt like a bunch of Eskimos, and I transported the skin (which weighed over fifty pounds) all the way to London to get it dressed as a usable hide. Unfortunately, it didn't stand up to the journey too well and cost me a substantial tip to a taxi driver for leaving a blubbery blood stain in the boot of his cab. Subsequently, it was completely spoiled in the processing and all our work, and the strange looks of people on the train, were for nothing.

A shopping trip to Whitley Bay produced a surprise, for on the way back along the beach I picked up an odd-looking fish. It had been gutted and thrown into the sea some time before as the tough, leathery skin had lost its colour, the eyes were sunken and some of the fins were worn and broken. Even so, unprepossessing as it appeared, its strange shape reminded me of trigger fish I had seen on television programmes about coral reefs. I took it back to the lighthouse, made some rough drawings and measurements, then skinned it (*Plate 19*). I salted the skin and threw the body out for the

MARCH 3rd

Puffin
Adult: winter plumage
washed ashore
Skate Road,
nr Holy Island
1st March

Puffin
Adult: breeding
washed ashore
Skate Road,
nr Holy Island
1st March

winglength: 171 mm
bill length: 48.7 mm
bill depth: 38.0 mm
tarsus: 28 mm

Little Auk ♂
winter plumage
washed ashore oiled
Blyth Beach
28th February

winglength: 129 mm
bill length: 15 mm

note dark underwing

(Plate 17)

CURLEW
St Mary's Island
March

Sketches of birds around the rocks –
the bird at the bottom of the page
was winkling crabs from among the
rockpools. It frequently turned its head
upside down to use its bill to fullest effect.

(Plate 18)

gulls. Here a chain of events begins, for a few days later I gave a copy of my notes about it to George, who passed these on to the Hancock Museum in Newcastle. I gave the skin to another friend in London, as he collects fish specimens, and thought little more about it. In the meantime, the Hancock Museum passed my notes on to the Fish Department at the Natural History Museum in London and they wrote to me asking whether I still had the specimen as they considered it to be something rarer than the usual trigger fish found in British waters. A telephone call put the Natural History Museum in touch with my fishy friend and he took the skin to them for a positive identification. Sure enough, the rather tattered creature proved to be a spotted trigger fish (*Canthidermis maculatus*), a tropical Atlantic species only unreliably recorded once before in British waters. Unfortunately, all the work and correspondence proved to be to no avail: because it had apparently been discarded from a passing fishing boat it could not be recorded as a truly authentic British specimen! Even so, it demonstrates the value of casual observations by amateur naturalists and gave me much encouragement to carry on collecting scraps of corpses!

MARCH 5th   My relief is arriving the day after tomorrow, so George and I had a last trip out this afternoon, and walked from St Mary's to Seaton Sluice, where there were no scoter but five goldeneye offshore. From there we went up Blyth Beach, but there were few birds around other than a nice party of four snow buntings by the watch-tower on the beach, feeding among the tideline debris and occasionally flying up with a delightful conversational twittering reminiscent of canaries. When we reached Blyth Harbour we soon found a flock of common gulls with a larger bird in their midst, and once again it proved to be a glaucous gull, this time a first-winter bird. It was getting misty as we caught the bus back home, and by the time I reached St Mary's Island, fog was rolling in off the sea and stayed throughout the evening.

MARCH 6th   Very thick fog all night. Continuing up to about 9.00 a.m. this morning brought several blackbirds and redwing attracted to the light just after midnight, but despite my efforts I was unable to catch any. When the fog lifted I counted over thirty blackbirds dotted around the lighthouse yard, and most of these soon drifted off towards the mainland as the visibility improved. One male blackbird was less fortunate for in the early afternoon he fell victim to a kestrel which came across from the mainland.

MARCH 7th   The morning was pretty well taken up by cleaning and tidying my quarters in readiness for the arrival of my relief, who eventually arrived in the late evening. I left St Mary's Island at 9.30 p.m. in the taxi that brought him.

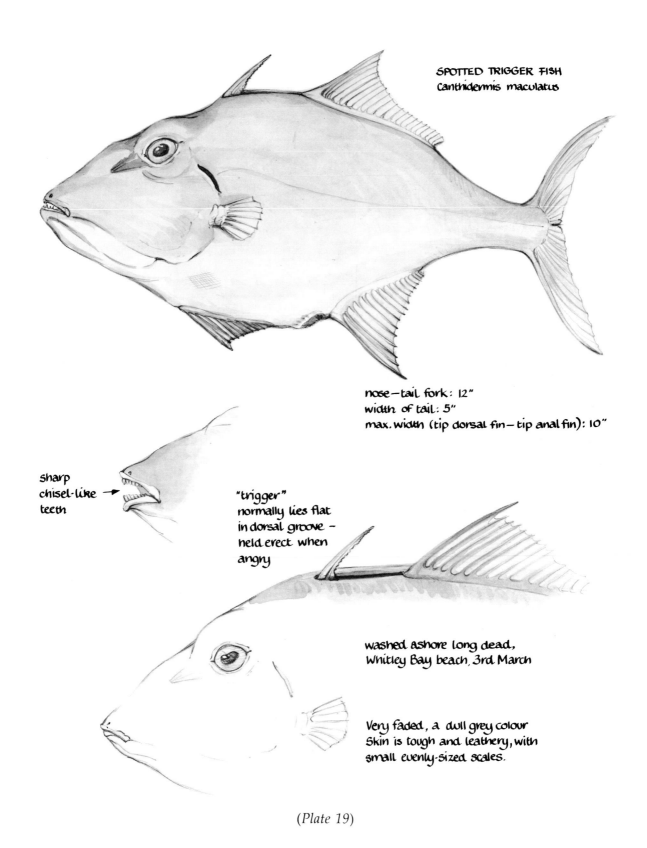

SPOTTED TRIGGER FISH
Canthidermis maculatus

nose—tail fork: 12"
width of tail: 5"
max. width (tip dorsal fin — tip anal fin): 10"

sharp
chisel-like →
teeth

"trigger"
normally lies flat
in dorsal groove —
held erect when
angry

washed ashore long dead,
Whitley Bay beach, 3rd March

Very faded, a dull grey colour
Skin is tough and leathery, with
small evenly-sized scales.

(Plate 19)

CROMER LIGHTHOUSE, NORFOLK
52° 56'N ; 1° 19'E

(Plate 20)

CROMER

I arrived at Cromer in Norfolk late in the evening of 21 March to spend a month as relief for the resident keepers who were taking two weeks of their annual leave consecutively. The lighthouse stands in a rather incongruous position at the edge of a golf course, about a half a mile from the cliff edge (*Plate 20*). The present octagonal tower was built in 1837, but a light was first exhibited from the cliffs in 1719. The rapid erosion of the soft boulder clay soil resulted in the original lighthouse falling into the sea in 1866, hence the modern station's situation so far from the edge. Danger from landslips may be very real, but no less serious is the danger from low-flying golf balls, some of which end up in the lighthouse garden!

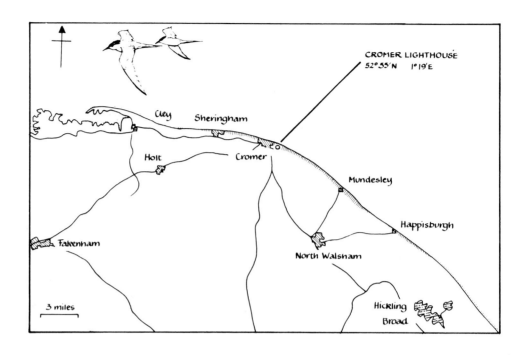

CROMER LIGHTHOUSE
52°55′N   1°19′E

Cley   Sheringham   Cromer   Holt   Mundesley   Happisburgh   Fakenham   North Walsham   Hickling Broad

3 miles

Cromer is a true land light, and only a mile or so from the town itself, so food presents few problems. Indeed, apart from the peculiar hours of work it is little different from any other job. Days free of duty provide a good opportunity to visit areas close by, and time could usually be found every day for a walk along the beach to indulge my curiosity about things washed ashore. Cromer has a special attraction in this respect, as it is one of the few places on the British coast where amber can be found and I spent much of my time on the beach hopefully picking up likely-looking pebbles. I had no luck and had to content myself with making a few drawings of pieces on display in the jeweller's window in Cromer! This lighthouse is quite popular with visitors, particularly school parties, but they seemed a bit disappointed that there is no fog signal, and surprised that it runs on mains electricity, with a stand-by generator for emergencies only.

The Norfolk coast in spring is exceptionally good for migrant birds, so I planned to spend most of my free time looking out for new arrivals.

MARCH 22nd   I spent part of the morning on the beach below the lighthouse, wandering up and down looking at some of the tideline debris. Showers of sleet and rain meant that apart from a group of about twenty energetic sanderling I had the shore to myself. Much of the rubbish was familiar, with the same old seaweeds, but more hornwrack than I had found before. This weed is characteristic of a sandy shoreline, but it isn't common on the west coast. The beach itself is a strange mix of sand and shingle with great patches of sticky clay where recent cliff falls have been eaten away by the tide. A dead guillemot was the only bird I found, but large numbers of dead sea-mice (*Aphrodite aculeata*) were lying along the most recent tideline (*Plate 21*). I counted at least thirty on a stretch about a mile long. These are strange, flattened marine worms rather like bits of tough gristle but with a brilliant fringe of iridescent spines along their sides. I don't know very much about their biology but they seem to be quite common along sandy shores, and they often turn up in the stomachs of dogfish.

The best find was a pipefish lying dead among weed on the shore. This was probably the greater pipefish (*Syngnathus acus*), which looks not unlike an elongated sea horse. They share similar breeding habits in that the female lays her eggs in a pouch on the male's belly, where he carries them until hatching. The individual I found proved to be a male, about ten inches long, complete with brood pouch, and was the first I had ever seen.

Early morning mist and drizzle produced a spectacular movement of birds MARCH 23rd heading inland. Between 6.00 a.m. and 8.30 a.m. I counted about 5,000 starlings in groups of 20 to 30, and over 250 brambling, mostly passing in fives and tens. It surprised me that there seemed to be no other species involved but from the comfort of the lantern, with the birds passing no more than 100 yards away, it was quite easy to be sure of identification. Mid-afternoon brought an improvement in the weather, so I walked along the beach for about two miles to Overstrand, looking for signs of the movement I watched in the morning. Sure enough I picked up five starlings in the tideline, and also remains of blackbird, redwing, fieldfare and brambling. Most surprising was a perfectly fresh red-legged partridge washed up by the tide and still warm (*Plate 22*). Groups of five or six live in the scrub around the cliff base and forage above the tideline. This bird was in immaculate condition, so I made a reference painting before turning it and the five starlings into study skins. On my way back I found the scattered remains of a male pintail, identifiable by its long tail feathers, which seemed to have been scavenged by a fox.

My first full day free of duty, so I decided to pay a visit to the marshes at MARCH 25th Cley, about ten or twelve miles up the coast. Public transport proved totally inadequate, so in the end I took up the offer of a lift from a local fisherman, on the way to visit his oyster beds at Thornham. He dropped me on the

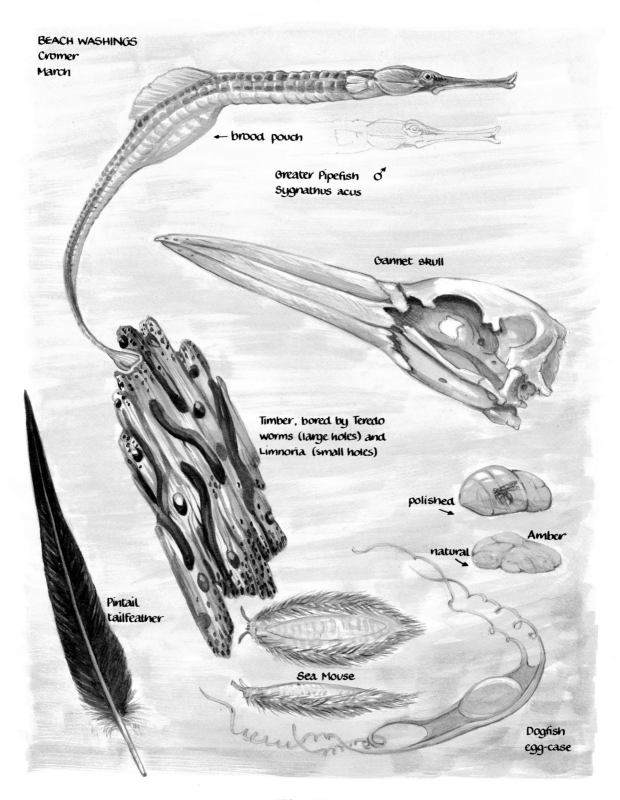

BEACH WASHINGS
Cromer
March

← brood pouch

Greater Pipefish ♂
Syngnathus acus

Gannet skull

Timber, bored by Teredo worms (large holes) and Limnoria (small holes)

polished

Amber

natural

Pintail tailfeather

Sea Mouse

Dogfish egg-case

(Plate 21)

REDLEGGED PARTRIDGE
Alectoris rufa
washed ashore
Cromer Beach
23rd March
immature ♀

winglength: 165 mm

no sign of injury

(Plate 22)

main road just by the reserve gate in the early afternoon and I soon reached a point from which I could look out over the reedy pools and flooded meadows. Almost immediately I heard, and then saw, a party of three bearded tits, flitting through the reeds in a narrow dyke, keeping low down and out of the wind. The pools held large numbers of dabbling duck, with over 200 shelduck, 100 wigeon, 70 each of mallard and teal, 20 gadwall and a pair of shoveler. Some of the birds were feeding, the wigeon grazing the wet grassland, while others dozed in the sun, sheltered from the cold wind by the reed-covered banks. The drakes were in fine plumage and many groups of birds were displaying, particularly the mallard and teal. The local female mallards should be on eggs by now, so most of the birds on the marsh were drakes.

The meadows held large numbers of lapwing and over a hundred golden plover, but the most striking bird of the day was a single black-tailed godwit in almost full summer plumage, probing among the grass for invertebrates (*Plate 23*). None of the black-tails I had seen in previous years were so far advanced into breeding plumage and its brilliant russet head, neck and flanks shone in the bright sun. I watched it for half an hour before it was startled by the sudden departure of a flock of neurotic golden plover and flew off across the marshes to be quickly lost from sight. Small numbers of black-tailed godwits breed in East Anglia and this may have been one of this population.

After such a superb bird everything else seemed an anti-climax, but I did witness a strange piece of behaviour on the part of a moorhen in a field along the road. For five minutes I watched it eating a dead drake mallard, which was lying among rough grass on the edge of a dyke. It seemed to have been freshly killed, but the moorhen pecked and pulled at it enthusiastically and swallowed several quite large pieces. I had never encountered carrion eating in moorhens before and it must surely be quite rare.

MARCH 26th

Very squally in the early morning, with winds north-west force five to six, easing after 3.00 p.m. to no more than force two to three. I had a brief walk along the beach (*Plate 24*), where I found oiled corpses of kittiwake, herring gull and yet another red-legged partridge! How these game birds end up in the sea is a mystery to me, but I imagine it has a lot to do with their escape tactics of flying quickly away and suddenly dropping down onto the ground. Possibly the odd bird makes a mistake and ends its escape flight by a drop in the sea.

Most unexpected this afternoon was a green woodpecker digging in an anthill on the lawn outside the lighthouse engine room for about twenty minutes. It eventually flew off towards the woods near Cromer church.

BLACK-TAILED GODWIT
Cley Marsh
25th March

Feeding in a wet meadow, wading ankle-deep
and probing with careful bill-thrusts.
Very richly coloured, in almost full summer
plumage.

(Plate 23)

MARCH 31st   With slightly better organisation, I managed to take full advantage of a day free of duty and reach Cley marsh by mid-morning. After the cold weather over the weekend some changes had taken place. Salthouse marsh held a fine adult whooper swan, looking conspicuous and rather uncomfortable in the midst of a couple of hundred teal all avidly guzzling in the wet meadow. Further down the marsh towards Cley I came across a greylag and a Brent goose grazing close together, but the large numbers of wigeon and other ducks seemed to be absent. Perhaps they had flown out to the mud banks of Blakeney Harbour. The long dyke leading down towards Cley village held a female red-breasted merganser, which caught two quite large eels during the time I watched it, but nothing else of great significance appeared, so I repaired to the George Inn for a substantial lunch and liquid refreshment. Suitably replete, I wandered aimlessly along the road to the south of the marsh and spent the time waiting for my bus in watching a big flock of golden plover feeding in the fields. Many of these were coming in to bright summer plumage and showed the black face and flanks typical of the northern race (*Plate 25*). Before too long I turned up another stranger in the shape of an elegant female ruff picking about in the wet grass. Eventually, my bus arrived and as we trundled off towards Cromer I had a tantalising glimpse of a bird of prey disappearing behind a clump of trees. I can only imagine it to have been a ring-tail hen harrier, but could not be certain. I had better luck at the bus stop, near Salthouse marsh, where a nice kingfisher perched on a branch overhanging the dyke alongside the road. It's a shame that bus companies don't provide for birdwatchers with unlimited request stops – many is the time that I've wished for a sudden breakdown as a rare bird rapidly disappears behind the speeding omnibus.

APRIL 4th   After a long bus trip involving a couple of changes, I reached Hickling Broad on a cold but sunny afternoon and followed a long embankment to the southern edge of the broad. The fields on either side of the track were full of snipe and I must have flushed over a hundred in the course of a mile or so. Most of the grazing meadows held pairs of redshank, some meadows two or three pairs, and many of these pairs were displaying to each other in between territorial squabbles with intruders. It seemed ages before I found a view of open water and for quite some time saw nothing more than great rafts of coot and the odd tufted duck and pochard. Eventually I came to a small bay sheltered from the snow flurries by alder trees and found a hundred or more teal along with six gadwall and a group of fifteen Bewick's swans picking over the weed in the shallow fringes. They seemed to be three discrete family groups of swans, consisting of male, female and three cygnets, and there was much posturing and flapping of wings whenever two families encroached on each other's feeding site. While I was watching the swans I noticed something crouching among the reeds at the water's

BLACKHEADED AND COMMON GULLS
Cromer Beach
March

Blackheaded Gull
1st-summer

Blackheaded Gull
adult, winter

note hint of
a ring on the
bill

Common Gull
winter

Common Gull
1st-summer

Blackheaded Gull
summer plumage

Common Gull
summer plumage

(Plate 24)

GOLDEN PLOVER AND RUFF

summer plumage
northern race

GOLDEN PLOVER

One or two of the "Goldies" are in full summer plumage - northern race birds showing a black face.

winter plumage

♀ RUFF quietly picking over a damp grassy patch. Very elegant, and noticeably small-headed.

(Plate 25)

EGYPTIAN GOOSE
Hickling Broad
4th April

A pair feeding in a field of
cereals. No apparent plumage
difference between the sexes.
assumed to be ♂ and ♀
because of their
proximity!

Kingfisher
Perched on a stump
along a dyke.

(Plate 26)

edge about thirty feet away, and realised that I was looking at a coypu which was staring straight back at me! How long it had been sitting there I can't say, but when it realised it had been spotted, it vanished with little more than a splash and a ripple. Coypu are South American rodents with a superficial resemblance to a rat, but nearer the size of a small terrier! They were first introduced as ranch animals to be bred for the fur trade (their pelts sold under the name of 'Nutria'), but escaped and established wild populations. They are largely aquatic, with webbed hind feet, and they found the Norfolk Broads much to their liking. Unfortunately, they are destructive to field crops such as sugar beet, and they also make large tunnels in the banks of dykes and ditches designed to contain the water in this flat landscape. As a consequence they are pretty unpopular and are trapped and shot wherever they occur, hence the shyness of the individual I saw. Cold weather causes high mortality among youngsters and this must help to some extent in keeping the population in check.

It proved to be quite a day for introduced species, for less than a mile from the coypu site I came upon a pair of Egyptian geese grazing quietly on a wet meadow (*Plate 26*). These striking birds were first introduced to East Anglia in the eighteenth century from Africa but unlike the coypu have never built up a large population and remain confined to a few sites in a small area of Norfolk. They were not particularly tame, and one bird, I think the female, kept throwing up her head and eyeing me suspiciously. After a few minutes she got up and flew about fifty yards further down the field, the male following closely. She seemed happier in this new position and both settled down to feed again, so I left them and made my way back to the main road, to hunt out a bus stop.

APRIL 6th   Despite an early morning frost the bright sunny weather persuaded me to take a walk up the beach in the continuing search for a spring migrant. Today finally produced not one, but two! The first indications of the arrival of some migrants came in the shape of several goldcrests, hunting insects in a gorse bush in the lighthouse garden at dawn. Then just after 7 a.m. I was watching a curlew on the golf course below the tower when a cock wheatear landed on the garden wall, and spent the next ten minutes or so feeding avidly among the tussocks on the edge of the fairway. The first summer migrant of the year, and a very handsome individual, boldly flashing his black and white tail and chivvying the meadow pipits which were feeding on the green. As if this wasn't a suitable harbinger of spring, a little later on I walked the beach as planned and found a female black redstart perched conspicuously on some rusted ironwork above the tideline.

I picked up a dead fulmar on the shore, which was in quite good condition so I spent the afternoon in making some drawings of it and preparing a study skin (*Plate 27*).

A chance meeting with another birdwatcher outside the lighthouse yesterday caused me to take a bus to Holt and then walk a couple of miles in sleet showers to a tiny hamlet called Hunworth where, I had been informed, a black-bellied dipper had wintered and was still in residence (*Plate 30*). After about four hours wandering up and down both banks of a two-mile stretch of river in the rain, I eventually found the bird sitting on a stone weir, looking about as wretched as I felt! Even so it was quite an event, for this is the continental race of the dipper and it probably doesn't occur more than once or twice a year in Britain. I made a few quick drawings with somewhat cramped and frozen fingers and retreated to a nice warm pub for a decent meal. The day also produced my third summer migrant for the year, in the shape of a chiffchaff flitting about in the pub garden, and probably far too cold to sing.

APRIL 8th

I had to receive a delivery of fuel oil this morning and then do some shopping in Cromer. It was gone eleven in the morning before I was free and as usual followed the beach into town, but did not find anything unusual apart from a dried and shrivelled pipefish by the pier. For a change of scenery I decided to come back along the cliff top and was most surprised to find a dead female water shrew lying on the path outside the coastguard station (*Plate 28*). I had always assumed this to be a species confined to the close proximity of fresh water, but here was a fresh corpse on the top of a cliff about 200 feet above sea level, and about a mile from the nearest pond. Still, I was very pleased to find an animal I had not had the chance to examine before, I took it back to the lighthouse and spent most of the afternoon drawing it and making it up as a study skin.

APRIL 10th

I was engrossed in this, sitting next to the open window facing the sea, when I became aware of a commotion among the many small birds which regularly feed around the lighthouse garden. Several blackbirds, a robin, a male wheatear and two or three jackdaws were all scolding and giving frantic alarm calls, so much so that eventually I found my binoculars and went to have a closer look. To my great surprise they were mobbing a large raptor which was sitting on an anthill about fifty yards from the tower, looking thoroughly fed up. Through the glasses it was plainly a rough-legged buzzard, and I watched it for the next ten minutes as it preened (*Plate 28*). Eventually it took off and flew over the golf course towards the south. I thought I had seen the last of it but about an hour later two rough-legs came back up the coast and circled over the lighthouse for a few minutes before drifting off north to be lost from sight over the sea. I managed to scribble some notes and sketches alongside the drawings of the water shrew.

FULMAR
Fulmaris glacialis
♀

washed ashore between
Cromer and Overstrand
6th April

In fair condition,
though rather thin.
A few small spots of
oil on the breast.
winglength: 322 mm
bill length: 37 mm
wingspan: ca. 36"

I made a study skin, which retained the
characteristic musty odour for many months.

(Plate 27)

ROUGH-LEGGED BUZZARD
Cromer
10th April

Sitting on a tussock on
the edge of the golf course.
Drawn from living-room
window at a range of
only 60 yards.

Eventually drifted away north east.

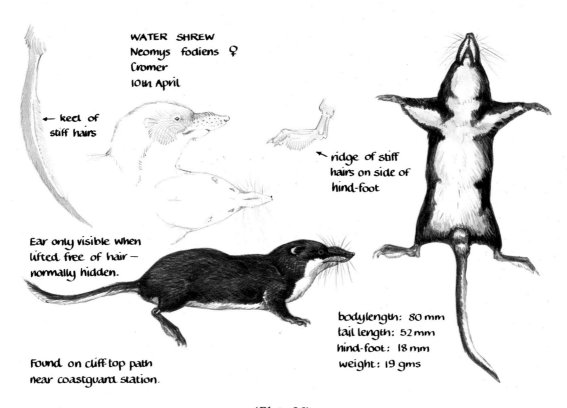

WATER SHREW
Neomys fodiens ♀
Cromer
10th April

← keel of
stiff hairs

← ridge of stiff
hairs on side of
hind-foot

Ear only visible when
lifted free of hair —
normally hidden.

body length: 80 mm
tail length: 52 mm
hind-foot: 18 mm
weight: 19 gms

Found on cliff-top path
near coastguard station.

(Plate 28)

APRIL 12th   Back again to Cley marsh, but the dull overcast weather seemed to influence the birds, as there was very little of note on most of the marsh. I did find a group of coypu feeding on floating vegetation. They seemed to be a female with two smaller youngsters, both of which were quite playful and kept climbing onto her flanks as she fed, and periodically jumped (or fell) back into the water with a splash. There was little more than a few Sandwich terns along the beach, until I reached the pools nearest to the road, and sat down to eat my lunch. After a little while two birds flew in across the marsh, and when they landed on the pools only fifty yards away it was plain to see that they were avocets. Perhaps they were part-way through a long journey, for they fed vigorously for ten minutes or so, scything their bills through the water to sift out invertebrates, and then after a thorough preen, they settled down to sleep. I took advantage of their closeness to make some sketches, and stayed watching them until the bus arrived (*Plate 29*).

APRIL 16th   At last a substantial change in the weather, with the wind moving round through west to south and a corresponding improvement in the weather. This brought a bonanza of migrants around the lighthouse, with eight or nine wheatears on the golf course, and a trickle of swallows and sand martins moving steadily along the coast. The real prize awaited discovery on the steep grassy cliffs, for when I went down for a walk along the tideline I noticed first one, and then at least four more, migrant ring ouzels flitting along the slopes (*Plate 30*) on their way to breeding grounds in the high moorland of Scotland and northern England after spending the winter in Africa and had stopped briefly to feed. They were bold and dashing swashbucklers, with a rich chackering call and much flirting and posturing in many ways reminiscent of fieldfares. In any case five together on a small stretch of cliff is quite an event, as I've walked for many miles in Snowdonia for the sight of a single one!

APRIL 18th   After drizzle and fog yesterday, a change of weather brought good numbers of spring migrants, with many swallows and sand martins moving north along the coast past the lighthouse. With only a couple of days before my turn of duty is over, I decided to pay a final trip to the marshes at Cley. The large numbers of wildfowl were absent, only fifty wigeon grazed the wet meadow near the main road, but out on the pools large numbers of shoveler were displaying, with many groups of six or seven drakes all trying to out-do each other (*Plate 30*). The gorse bushes along the road were alive with willow warblers and chiffchaffs newly arrived from Africa, the morning much enlivened by their songs. So many small migrants always leads me to

AVOCETS
Cley Marshes
12th April

(Plate 29)

RING OUZEL
Cromer
16th April
a group of six on the cliffs

FIRECRESTS
Cley
18th April

BLACKBELLIED DIPPER
Hunworth, nr Holt
8th April
The continental form,
it has spent most
of the winter on
the small river
at Hunworth.

(Plate 30)

SPOTTED REDSHANK AND GREENSHANK
Cley Marsh
18th April

Spotted Redshank

Greenshank

Both these birds were feeding
in muddy pools on the marshes.
They show signs of summer plumage,
the Spotshank blotched sooty brown,
the Greenshank with a few dark
feathers and arrow-shaped marks
on the flanks.

(Plate 31)

hope for something out of the ordinary, and I eventually found two firecrests feeding quietly in a small bush behind one of the hides in the reserve. They were very tame, and as I sat and watched they came so close that I could no longer focus my binoculars on them! Some cattle were grazing out on the marshes, surrounded by dozens of yellow wagtails, the males so vivid that they seemed to glow a rich buttercup yellow. I searched for continental blue-headed birds but didn't see one, although there seemed to be groups of birds arriving and departing all the time, and I'm sure that during the half-hour I spent watching them over a hundred must have gone by me. The big plover flocks I had watched on my previous visits had dwindled to about twenty, most now gaining summer plumage, but apart from these, waders seemed rather thin on the ground. I did find a greenshank feeding in the pools, already showing signs of summer plumage, with a few bold black feathers in its mantle and nice arrow-shaped marks on its flanks, but the only other worthy of note was a spotted redshank wading elegantly in the deeper water by a sluice gate (*Plate 31*). This was also showing traces of breeding plumage, but in a rather more erratic way which left it randomly blotched sooty-brown! It seemed to be having much more success than the greenshank which was picking about in the shallows, while the spotted redshank darted about chasing tiny fish and fast-moving crustaceans.

I had received the offer of a lift, provided I was by the coastguard station at 3.00 p.m., so I ate my sandwiches while sitting on the shingle nearby. All the time I sat there a steady procession of Sandwich terns flapped west, each small group calling raucously (*Plate 32*). By the time my lift arrived (fortunately a little late!) I had counted 120 birds, and a brief stop in Sheringham on the way home showed still more working along the coast in the typically purposeful flight of birds on migration. I wondered whether these might be local birds from the colony at Scolt Head or perhaps from the colonies of Scotland and northern England. Some may have been on their way to Coquet Island where I had spent a fruitful, if ternless, January!

APRIL 20th   My last day at Cromer, spent in packing my gear and tidying up my quarters. I did manage a brief look along the beach during the afternoon, and succeeded in finding three ring ouzels along the cliffs. Swallows and sand martins were constantly moving along the coast towards the north-west and so many linnets went past me that I kept losing count. There were lots of wheatears on the golf course and while I watched the fulmars displaying on their muddy ledges near Overstrand, two house martins flicked past. The warm sun had obviously had an effect on the insect population for on the walk back along the cliff path I saw three peacock butterflies, four small tortiseshells and one vivid sulphur-yellow brimstone.

SANDWICH TERNS
City Beach
18th April

A large passage of Sandwich Terns
heading north for most of the day.
A few small groups settled on the
beach near the coastguard look-out
for about twenty minutes.

The strident "kirrick" calls of flying birds
give advance warning of their approach,
and must serve to keep groups together.

(Plate 32)

SOUTH BISHOP, PEMBROKESHIRE
51° 51′ N; 5° 25′ W

(Plate 33)

SOUTH BISHOP

On my return from Cromer I received notification from Trinity House that I had been promoted to Assistant Keeper and appointed to South Bishop lighthouse off the Pembrokeshire coast (*Plate 33*). This meant I would join the permanent crew of that station, and for a while at least my wandering about had finished. I couldn't have asked for a better station, for South Bishop is one of my local lights. A short drive up the coast from my parents' house and I could see it standing on top of the rock far out across St Bride's Bay. I knew from the old copy of *Birds of Pembrokeshire* I possessed that it had been notorious for attracting birds around the turn of the century but no one I spoke to knew much about it today.

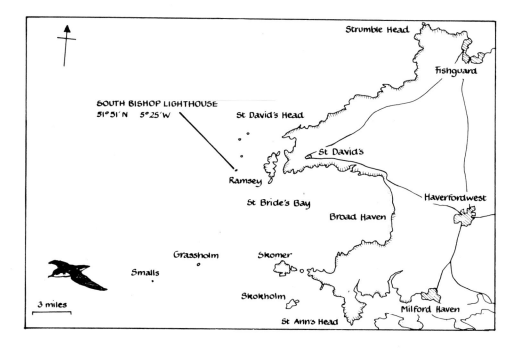

The lighthouse itself stands on a substantial piece of volcanic rock, about 200 yards long, 100 yards wide, rising about 100 feet above sea-level. The tower is rather short, only about 36 feet high, although the light is 143 feet above mean high-water level. The station was built in 1839 and is unusual in that the living accommodation is in a conventionally-shaped house. The whole station is surrounded by a wall, and is strikingly white with black roofs. The accommodation was designed for two families, but it seems unlikely that any other than lightkeepers ever lived here, for it is a very exposed station and the sea sometimes floods the courtyard and breaks the lower windows of the houses.

This stretch of the coast has the most marvellous atmosphere, the quality of the light is such that on a clear day the mainland seems to stand out, sharp and clear, as if it were only an arm's length away. In addition, in late summer an offshore wind brings the unmistakable smells of sweet grass and hay-making out to the lighthouse. Unfortunately, during the hot summer of 1976 the smell was often that of wood smoke and ash, for extensive gorse fires ravaged the mainland clifftops.

The light exhibited from South Bishop is by far the most powerful I have ever worked with. It has an intensity of 576,000 candle-power, a range of twenty-four miles and shows a single white flash every five seconds. It is this combination of range and brightness which makes it so fatally attractive to migrant birds and I was to find it a consistently good place for birdwatching. I decided to keep accurate figures of the numbers of migrants recorded, and to ring as many birds as I could. In fact I followed a system of log-books and standard recording forms identical to those used by British bird observatories. I hoped to be able to increase my knowledge of aspects of natural history other than birds by making careful observations and notes of what went on around me.

The helicopter relief mustered at St Ann's Head lighthouse, only seven or eight miles from home, so I felt truly a part of the local coastal community, the more so as most of the fishing boats I would see around the coast belonged to family friends! I reported to the depot at Swansea on May 15th and we mustered at St Ann's the next day to fly out to South Bishop (*Plate 34*).

Basil, Tony and I arrived on station by helicopter just before midday, and for the next three hours or so were completely absorbed in the normal relief day chores of unpacking food and personal gear, stowing the safety and fire-fighting equipment from the landing pad and checking the generators, light gear and radio. These last are in a way unnecessary as the departing crew always makes sure that they are left in first-class order, with any defects carefully noted, but it is a little ritual of arrival which even unsuperstitious lightkeepers carry on.

MAY 16th–17th

Eventually the jobs were done and I went out for a good look around. The gully below the living room is rich green with new growth of scurvy-grass and I found a few small warblers feeding there. All seemed to be chiffchaffs, flitting among the vegetation and occasionally catching small insects from the rocky wall. One bird was even singing from the aerial wire, despite the seemingly inhospitable surroundings of this bare rock. The gully on the western side of the island is even more barren, with no vegetation to speak of, and the single male whitethroat which 'churred' at me from the slopes was having a hard time trying to skulk among the rocks. He was a particularly smart bird, with a rich pink breast and blue-grey head setting off his white throat very well.

The rocks below the tower produced several unfortunate migrants which had been killed at the light during the previous night, and I collected nine after a brief but careful search. Five were sedge warblers, streaky brown with cream eye-stripes, the others were a spotted flycatcher, a whitethroat, a willow warbler and a grasshopper warbler (*Plate 35*). All had completed the long and dangerous journey from Africa to die on this isolated rock so close to their destination. Meeting the little tragedies of migration like this tend to leave me awestruck at the force which drives small birds to undertake such monumental journeys, not once, but twice a year.

When I made them into study skins later in the evening I found that every

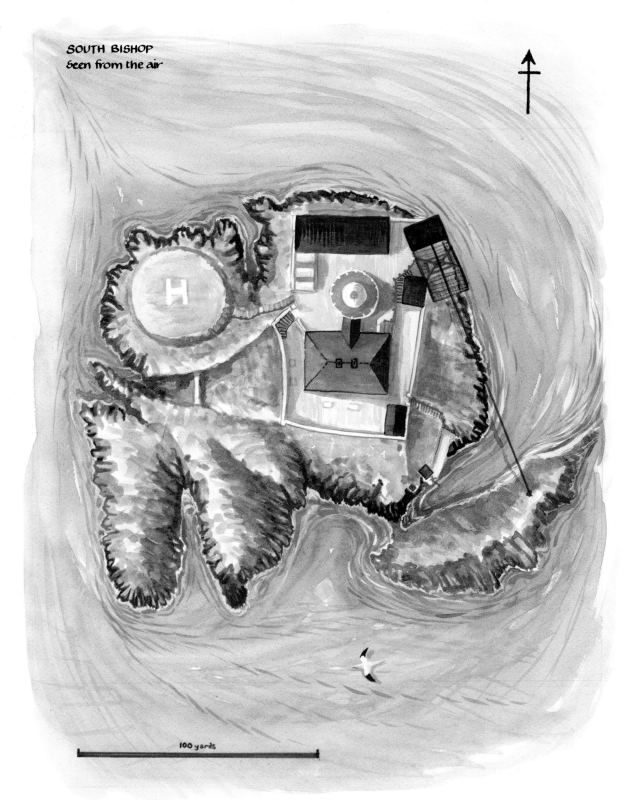

SOUTH BISHOP
Seen from the air

H

100 yards

(Plate 34)

SMALL MIGRANTS KILLED AT THE LIGHT
South Bishop
Spring

Grasshopper Warbler
16th May
wing: 60mm
weight: 13.1 gms

Willow Warbler
16th May
wing: 63 mm
weight: 9.1 gms

Sedge Warbler
16th May
wing: 64 mm
weight: 10.7 gms

note broad bill
and rictal bristles

Spotted Flycatcher
16th May
wing: 82 mm
weight: 13.0 gms

Chiffchaff
20th May
wing: 63 mm
weight: 8.0 gms

(Plate 35)

one was very light, devoid of all body fat, the essential fuel for long distance flights.

Looking down from the tower in the late afternoon I noticed a dark object stuck in the guttering of the annexe. As water from the roof tops is collected for domestic use, blockages are cause for concern, so I brought a step-ladder and went up to remove it. Imagine my surprise when the lump bit me, and then scuttled off down the gutter! Eventually, with Tony's help, I fished out an indignant Manx shearwater, which I ringed and then put in a cardboard box for release after dark. Shearwaters are best thought of as miniature albatrosses, and during the summer they breed in thousands on the islands of Skomer and Skokholm, only eight or ten miles south across St Bride's Bay. They come into their nest burrows after dark to avoid predation by great black-backed gulls and as a result crash landings by shearwaters are a regular feature of the summer months on South Bishop. We let this one go at dusk, and the following morning found a different (unringed) one under a fuel tank (*Plate 36*). This we kept in a cardboard box in the storeroom, and during the afternoon I made a page of drawings of it as it sat on the floor. The strength of their long hooked beaks is only apparent when they bite, as they seem to at every opportunity. It is a real bite too, nothing so feeble as a peck, the bird taking a good beakful of flesh and then shaking it wildly so that the sharp hook at the tip draws blood practically every time. With their large dark eyes and smart black and white plumage shearwaters are handsome birds, and at sea they fly with all the dash and grace of their larger South Atlantic cousins. I had ringed many hundreds on Skomer in previous years and they are firmly among my favourite birds.

A steady trickle of migrants has passed through, mostly odd wheatears and a few willow warblers and chiffchaffs. I caught a female wheatear at the light in the early morning of 17 May, and released it, ringed, at dawn.

MAY 20th

A pair of oystercatchers has made South Bishop their home, displaying frequently and noisily on the rocky plateau by the helipad, and chasing the larger gulls mercilessly. Today they were more noisy than usual, one bird, presumably the male, was dive-bombing the herring gulls so much that I could only conclude there to be a nest on the island. In the afternoon I spent an hour or so searching the level rocky patches they most frequently use, and although I found a depression lined with small stones between two outcrops, the oystercatchers seemed unconcerned, and I gave up my search. Later in the afternoon I went to sit on the rocks below the fog signal, a vantage point from which I could see the tide race to the west of the island. Good numbers of shearwaters gather in this area towards dusk, prior to going in to their burrows and provide a great spectacle as they sweep past in long lines, skimming the surface of the waves, often backlit by the rays of

the setting sun. After I had been sitting there for about twenty minutes a terrific commotion started up from the cliff edge below my feet and beyond my vision. It was plainly an oystercatcher, and as I advanced gingerly down the slope it flew away from a narrow ledge and out across the helipad. Sure enough, the ledge held a shallow nest scrape with one large egg, creamy white with darker spotting. It isn't surprising that the birds were unconcerned by my searches over the rocky plateau, for the nest was here on the edge of a thirty-foot cliff! Needless to say, I stopped using that particular spot for sea-watching, and a couple of days later when I checked again, the bird was sitting on two eggs.

A small group of gulls circling over the water attracted my attention to a dark object floating in the tide stream this morning, and as the sea was flat calm I waited to see what it was that caused the excitement. It drifted by about twenty yards out from the boat landing and there was no mistaking it; a dead donkey. I watched until it was out of sight, only the solitary herring gull sitting on its flanks to show where it was. There had been a number of articles on the television and in magazines recently about the horsemeat trade, and in particular the live export of ponies and donkeys from Ireland, for slaughter abroad. One of the pictures showed a dead horse being thrown overboard, and I wondered whether this unfortunate donkey had come from such a ship. If so, it had at least been spared the stress of a long sea voyage, but for the next few days I looked at passing ships with fresh eyes, wondering which of them, if any, carried this sad cargo.

MAY 22nd

A shoal of tiny fish moved into the slack water in the lee of the rock this morning, the shimmering of their silver flanks was plainly visible through the clear water as they moved in unison. I was surprised at how easy it was to pick them out, and so it was only to be expected that large numbers of auks, shearwaters and gulls quickly gathered to take advantage of the situation. The auks, mostly razorbills, but a few guillemots among them, dived expertly, and I could see them 'flying' underwater, flapping their wings steadily as they pursued the tiny fish. The air trapped in their dense feathers made them shine like silver torpedoes and it was remarkable how quickly the water ran off the oily plumage when they surfaced. Shearwaters adopted a different and rather more spectacular mode of attack, 'plunge-diving' into the sea from the air and quickly taking to the wing to try again a little further on. The gulls also used this method, but their greater buoyancy made it much more laborious and they hardly seemed to submerge at all, but bobbed up quickly like corks. The herring gulls frequently resorted to

MAY 25th

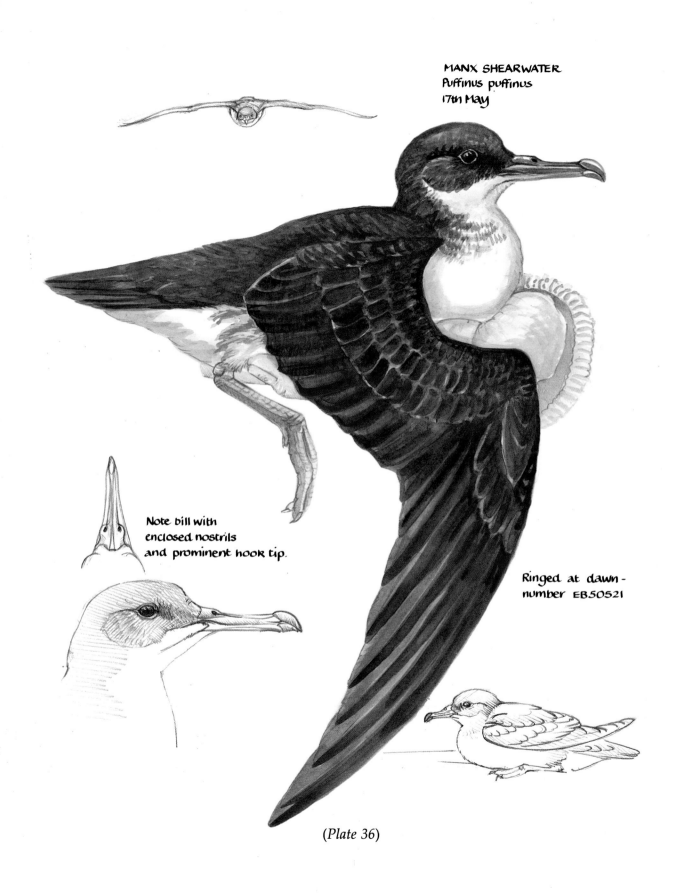

MANX SHEARWATER
Puffinus puffinus
17th May

Note bill with
enclosed nostrils
and prominent hook tip.

Ringed at dawn -
number EB50521

(Plate 36)

SOUTH BISHOP
May

Only three plant species are widespread
on South Bishop, drawn here as isolated
clumps, although Rock Spurrey carpets
some of the sheltered areas, and Scurvy
Grass grows in dense tangles on the
sheltered east slope.

1 Thrift
   (Armeria maritima)

2 Common Scurvy Grass
   (Cochlearia officionalis)

3 Rock Sea Spurrey
   (Spergularia rupicola)

♂ Wheatear

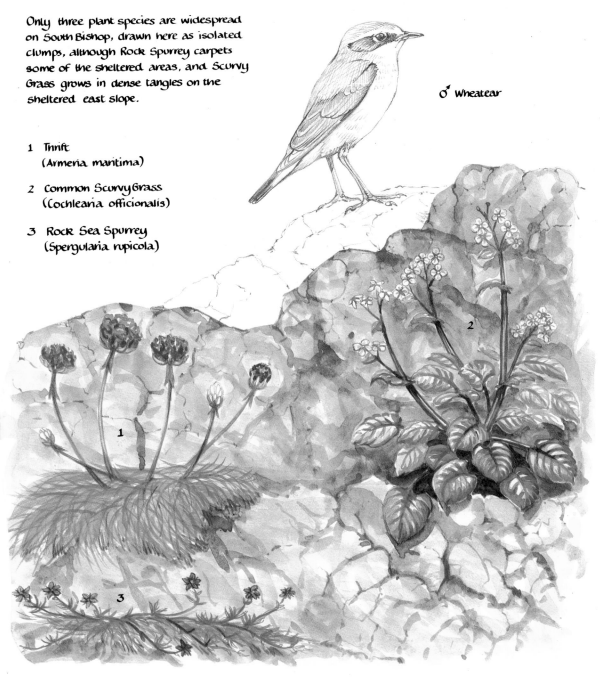

(Plate 37)

stealing fish from the auks and shearwaters, who were easily intimidated and didn't resist, so for half an hour this small area of sea was a frothy mêlée of frantically diving and flapping seabirds.

Spring migration continues, but the persistent east and north-easterly winds keep the level of activity to no more than a trickle. Every morning brings something new, but only one or two individuals, an occasional wheatear (*Plate 37*) or whitethroat, a few willow warblers or chiffchaffs. They stay a day or two and move on. Some stop only for a few minutes, turtle doves seldom do more than drink before continuing their journeys with erratic flicking wing-beats. Whimbrels pass over, often just a trilling call from the dark night sky. Occasionally fog or drizzle brings them down to rest on the rocks below the helipad. Curlews in a similar situation pick among the weedy low tide pools for crabs, but the whimbrel find nothing to their liking and soon move on. The most unexpected visitors have been the tree sparrows, odd ones and twos turning up on several days to pick over the kitchen scraps before quickly moving on. What they are doing on a bleak little rock at least six miles from the nearest copse or spinney is anybody's guess. I don't think they can rightly be considered migrants and their appearance, no matter how charming, leaves me puzzled.

MAY 29th   The most significant feature has been the steady passage of swallows, sand and house martins northwards across the sea. Little groups of five or six, mostly swallows, pass by the island every five or ten minutes, and occasionally a larger group comes up across St Bride's Bay from Skomer and flicks past the lighthouse heading arrow-straight towards Bardsey and beyond. The direct purposeful flight is quite unlike the leisurely way swallows dally over fields and lakes during the summer and there is no mistaking the intention of birds sticking to the course that will take them home. Surprisingly this passage seems to continue after dark to some extent, for today I caught a house martin at the light just after 1 a.m.; when I released it at dawn, after ringing, it took off towards the north with no hesitation.

JUNE 4th   An adult herring gull was sitting on the yard wall when I went out this morning and it didn't take me long to realise that he was a bit poorly, with one leg missing below the knee. When I threw him some kitchen scraps he wolfed them down and immediately looked around for some more. Over the next few days we kept him supplied with bits and pieces, and gradually he got better, until he was making short flights down to the rocky pools to fish and bathe. He didn't forget us altogether, and occasionally came back for a hand-out. How did he know that we would be a soft touch?

Fog and mist over the past week has kept most birds grounded, although **JUNE 10th** we have been visited by odd warblers from time to time. Today saw a bit of an improvement in the weather and as a result we had a few more small birds around, including another tree sparrow and a couple of spotted flycatchers. Gannets were fishing off the boat landing this afternoon, diving into the sea with terrific force. I marvel at the way they can avoid hitting others already on the water, for such a collision would surely prove fatal to one or both the birds.

Relief day. Calm bright and sunny, with no wind. It isn't often that relief **JUNE 13th** day weather is near perfect, so we were pretty fortunate, despite this being Friday 13th! The helicopter arrived to pick us up, and as we flew back across St Bride's Bay towards St Ann's, we flew over a group of gannets collecting seaweed from the surface of the water. I presume they were taking it back to their nest sites on Grassholm, but I couldn't be sure.

JULY 11th

Very warm and sunny with a sea haze cutting visibility down to a couple of miles. There were two dead swifts lying below the aerial mast, and after we had finished unpacking I went down the steps and picked them up. They had been killed a few days previously and were a bit smelly but I made a series of sketches and colour notes before I skinned them (*Plate 38*). They were both adult, their dark greeny-black feathers rather worn at the edges after a hectic breeding season. I hadn't expected to find swifts killed at the light, not thinking of them as night migrants.

Heavy rain just before dawn cleared fairly early, leaving a fresh south- **JULY 14th** westerly wind and a heavy swell rolling over the rocks below the helipad. Visibility was very good, and after finishing the weather log at 9 a.m. I sat watching a steady procession of Manx shearwaters moving towards Skomer. They were passing very close by my perch, skimming the waves and banking off towards the south, giving tremendous views of the crisp black and whiteness of their plumage and the subtle changes of wing-angle as they flap and glide over the water. Suddenly I noticed two shearwaters moving quickly southwards about fifty yards offshore. They were bigger than the Manx, with longer wings, and were strikingly brown and white in bright sun. They both had prominent black caps and dark tails, with obvious white collars and less visible white rump patches. These were

SWIFT
Apus apus
South Bishop

Body tough and cylindrical

Adult
killed at the light
11th July

winglength: 171 mm
bill length: 7·3 mm

I was surprised to find these birds killed at the light,
not having supposed them to be night migrants.

Immature
killed at the light
very fat
6th August

winglength: 169 mm
bill length: 6·7mm

wingspan of adult: ca. 16"

(Plate 38)

undoubtedly great shearwaters (*Plate 39*). Although they are regular autumn visitors to the Irish coast very few turn up in west Wales. They breed in the south Atlantic on the Tristan da Cunha group of islands and have a complex migration pattern which takes them up the east coast of America and across the north Atlantic to the Irish coast and Biscay, returning along the same route during late August and September. They were soon lost to sight, leaving me with a half page of scribbled notes and shaky sketches to record the event. Later in the day I worked these up into something a bit more presentable, and consulted my reference books on one or two points which rather puzzled me. I had always imagined (from the textbook description) that great shearwaters would be grey-brown or grey, but these birds were markedly brown above, showing lighter scalloping probably caused by pale feather margins.

Both pairs of rock pipits on the island are busy feeding young, as shown by JULY 15th
their continual jaunts back and forth with beaks full of invertebrates (*Plate 40*). One pair has a nest in a totally inaccessible crack thirty feet above the waters of the boat landing. Until today I didn't know where the other was, but suspected from the activity that it was on the rocky slope below the winch room, in a small crevice in the rocks, practically obscured by rough grass. With the aid of a piece of driftwood which served as a ladder, I was able to reach it and extract three partially-grown youngsters, which I quickly put back after ringing. A short while later I sat in the winch room and watched the adults coming and going, just to reassure myself that they hadn't been put off by my interference with the nest site. A week or so later these chicks had fledged, and were feeding among the weedy pools in company with the juveniles from the other nest.

Common porpoises are regular visitors to the Pembrokeshire coast, JULY 17th
particularly in midsummer. They are especially attracted to shoaling mackerel, their glossy-black backs and hooked dorsal fins often appearing amidst flocks of frantically diving gannets. Calm summer days with a glassy sea rolling languidly around the rocks provide ideal conditions for spotting porpoises and today groups of five and seven passed by. As a rule they keep a fair distance away from the rock so I was a bit surprised to see three lying calmly in the waters of the boat landing. But these were no common porpoise! They were dull-grey rather than black, with a much elongated body, a blunt snout, sharply curved dorsal fin and peculiar white 'scars' in swirling patterns over their backs convinced me that they were Risso's dolphin (*Plate 41*). Although they are not uncommon these were the first I had seen. They lay wallowing comfortably in the water, occasionally blowing a fine spray from their nostrils. Two were large, measured against

the boat landing later they must have been in excess of ten feet long, the other was rather smaller, only half their length, and I assumed it to be a youngster. This one kept splashing about, half-rolling on its back flicking water with its narrow flippers, until one of the adults moved slowly closer and gave it a sideways nudge with its head. This did the trick, and the youngster settled down to cruise impatiently around the boat landing, while the adults looked as if they were enjoying the sun-warmed water. After several minutes both adults blew great clouds of vapour into the air, and with no apparent effort cruised steadily out of the boat landing and away to the north-west, the youngster occasionally splashing the surface noisily with its tail flukes. Was it an inexperienced swimmer, or playing the goat?

JULY 26th

Last night, as the sun was going down, a single heron flapped slowly past the lighthouse and continued westwards until it was lost to sight. I was a bit surprised to see this purposeful expression of the migrating instinct in a bird I had never imagined to move across the Irish sea, but this morning two immatures followed the same ponderous course, followed only a few minutes later by a group of three. Unfortunately, the hazy conditions meant that I couldn't tell the age of this last group, but all these birds disappeared towards the western horizon and so I spent the greater part of the day keeping an eye open for signs of others moving west, or these intrepid individuals coming back.

My vigilance produced no more herons, but I was rewarded by a fine male peregrine which circled the island a couple of times before making off towards Grassholm. Three-quarters of an hour later a little group of six starlings came in from the west hotly pursued by the same peregrine! He made a few playful stoops at the little group, but I don't think he was deadly serious, as he broke off to circle the island, leaving the starlings to continue hastily on towards the mainland. Eventually the peregrine also made off towards Ramsey, but his playful mood continued, and he made a couple of dummy passes at earnest, heavily-laden gannets returning to Grassholm from the fishing grounds off St David's Head.

By midday the wind had dropped to nil, and the rising temperatures persuaded me to take my fishing rod down to the boat landing and try for some mackerel, but as they didn't respond at all, I was soon reduced to sitting on the rocks watching the kittiwakes feeding in the tide race between South Bishop and Ramsey. The flat calm sea curled gently around the rocks, making barely a sound, so I was a bit surprised to hear a gentle splashing coming from the boat landing. When I stood up to see what was making this unexpected noise, I saw a strange fish on the surface. It was about the size of a dustbin lid and was lying on its side gently flapping its dorsal and anal fin in and out of the water. I was delighted to see this unlikely-looking

GREAT SHEARWATERS
Puffinus gravis
South Bishop
14th July

Passed by ca. 50 yards offshore
at 0920 BST.

These wash drawings are a compilation
of the sketches made at the time, which
were very brief. Both birds were grey-brown,
with prominent dark caps and tails.

Manx Shearwater

The dark "shoulder mark", reminiscent of
a Black Tern, was noticeable.

(Plate 39)

ROCK PIPITS
South Bishop

nest site in
rock crevice
below the
engine room

These nestlings were
ringed on 15th July,
when they were
about six days old.
ring numbers:
B3 87705 - 06 - 07

All successfully fledged
about a week later,
and were feeding along
the tideline.

Adult
bringing
food

(Plate 40)

COMMON PORPOISE AND RISSO'S DOLPHIN
South Bishop
July

Common Porpoise (Phocoena phocoena) is the commonest
cetacean (whale-like animal) on the Pembrokeshire coast,
and can sometimes be seen in schools of twenty to
thirty, although threes and fours are more usual.

Risso's Dolphin (Grampus griseus)
is rather more rare. This trio came
close enough for sketches on 17th July.
Note the hooked dorsal fin, in
contrast to the porpoise's triangular
one, and also Risso's longer fore-flippers.

When they are basking near
the surface the white "scars"
along the back are quite prominent.

(Plate 41)

creature, a sunfish, for it is a relatively rare fish in British waters, occasionally turning up during hot summers, drifting in from the Atlantic (*Plate 42*). They are most peculiar fish, with no obvious tail, long paddle-like fins, and a tiny mouth. This habit of lying on the surface basking in the sun gives them their name, but few people ever see them do it. They spawn in the Sargasso Sea along with our European eels, and apparently produce prodigious quantities of eggs, something like 300 million per female! After a few minutes it suddenly righted itself, adopting a more conventional fishy posture and swam steadily out into the tide race, dorsal fin still flapping from side to side just above the surface, until it vanished in the broken water of the flooding tide.

AUGUST 2nd   The past two nights have seen a number of small migrants attracted to the light, last night over fifty were flitting around in the beams. Fortunately very few have been killed, only a couple of willow warblers and a sedge warbler, but I have managed to catch and ring half a dozen warblers and a shearwater. The gentle easterly winds and hazy conditions have brought a bonanza of insects, including many wasps, ladybirds and a smattering of butterflies, including large whites and peacocks (*Plate 43*). During the attractions at night several moths have come to the lantern, but the only species I have found during the day were a few large yellow underwings, hiding on the rough timbers of the storeroom, and a single magpie moth found dead on the gallery.

A very large bull seal turned up on the haul-out opposite the boat landing this morning, but he kept his distance from the little group of cows which is normally around. He seemed to have a large white spot almost encircling the back of his neck, and I was amazed when I looked through my binoculars to see that it was a massive open wound which seemed to have removed most of the skin from his neck. It wasn't bleeding, but had been washed clean by the sea water (*Plate 43*). As I watched, a turnstone which was feeding nearby wandered up, pulled off and ate a piece of tissue which was hanging loosely from the edge of the wound. The bull didn't react and I thought he must be very ill, but later on I saw him swimming around the southern end of the island, later still he was eating a dogfish in the boat landing! His wound is difficult to explain, for this is not a time of year associated with aggression in seals. He was also one of the biggest bulls I have ever seen, so whoever (or whatever) injured him must have been very big indeed. He disappeared after a few days and I did not see him again.

AUGUST 3rd   Visitors today! We had a radio call from the Air-Sea Rescue station at Brawdy this morning asking for permission to land R.A.F. personnel on our

SUNFISH
Mola mola
26th July

About the diameter of a dustbin lid,
perhaps two feet across. A dull,
leathery greeny-brown colour,
with paler underside and dark fins.

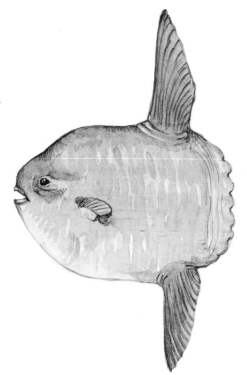

It first attracted my attention
by splashing with one fin while
lying just below the surface

note: this is apparently a tiddler,
the maximum size recorded is over
10 feet long, weighing 1½ tonnes.

When it adopted a more
conventional fishy posture
the dorsal fin flopped from
side to side in an uncontrolled
manner.

(Plate 42)

Yellow underwings
(Noctua pronuba)

Peacock Butterfly
(Inachis io)

Sevenspot Ladybird
(Coccinella 7-punctata)
magnified x 2

Magpie Moth
(Abraxas grossulariata)

The very large bull seal as I first saw
him, hauled out on the rocks by the
boat landing, showing his severe wound.

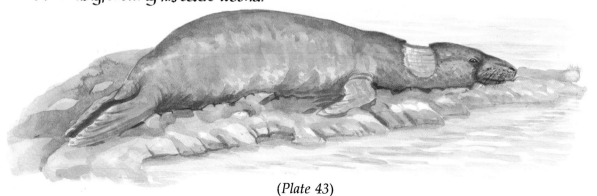

(Plate 43)

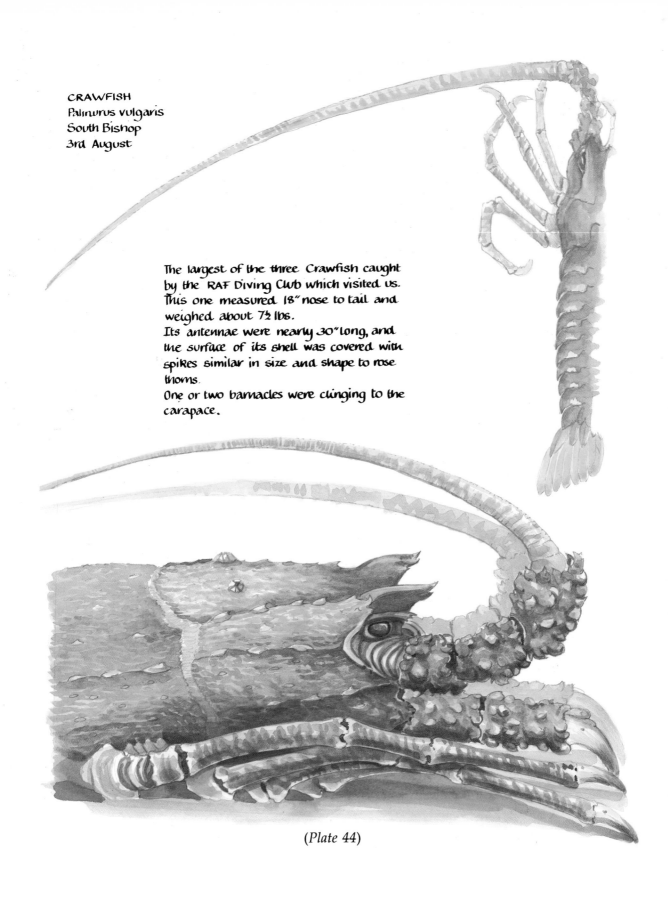

CRAWFISH
Palinurus vulgaris
South Bishop
3rd August

The largest of the three Crawfish caught
by the RAF Diving Club which visited us.
This one measured 18" nose to tail and
weighed about 7½ lbs.
Its antennae were nearly 30" long, and
the surface of its shell was covered with
spikes similar in size and shape to rose
thorns.
One or two barnacles were clinging to the
carapace.

(Plate 44)

helipad. It seemed that an R.A.F. diving club from a base in the West Country was visiting Pembrokeshire, and was keen to dive in some new territory. We gladly gave our permission and consequently spent the day surrounded by the paraphernalia of diving, sharing our island with eight or nine strangers! It was interesting to hear their comments on the undersea world around the rock. All agreed that the visibility was vastly superior to anything they had encountered closer inshore and that there were very large shoals of pollack as well as good numbers of dogfish. They brought up about a dozen edible crabs and three large crawfish, the biggest weighing over eight pounds (*Plate 44*). I felt rather sorry for these thorny sea-monsters at the time, but when our visitors came to leave they gave us the biggest and that evening we enjoyed crawfish and salad with mayonnaise. I defy anyone to tell it from a lobster on the plate!

AUGUST 5th   Just after midnight last night an electrical storm developed, moving slowly past on light southerly winds. This was my first experience of lightning on a lighthouse and apart from an uncomfortable feeling of exposure it was quite exhilirating. The brightness of the flashes surprised me, for they lit up the coastline of Ramsey and the rocky headland beyond as if it was daylight but all washed in a ghostly blue-grey against a black sky. The effect of the lightning on the Manx shearwaters was memorable. As it developed they came flicking past the light ever faster, with more and more birds as the storm reached its height. At this point the sky was a mêlée of rapidly moving bodies and chortling cries, all seeming intent on passing as close to the light as possible. Inevitably many hit the glazing or aerial wires, and I worked up quite a sweat trying to catch them. It surprised me that many of those which hit the tower and fell onto the flat engine room roof recovered quickly and flew away before I could catch them, indeed the entire night's episode produced only one dead shearwater, which had flown into the radio beacon aerial and showed the mark of the wire clearly across its throat. At 1.00 a.m. it began to rain heavily and this ended the shearwater circus abruptly. I had ten birds to ring, all locked in the store shed while I waited to see which would recover from concussion. By 1.30 a.m. the rain had eased slightly and I went out to examine and ring them. They were all fine, and when I released them one at a time they flew off strongly towards Skomer. As I was shutting the shed door I looked up at the lantern and saw a small bird fluttering at the glazing; when I reached the gallery there was a storm petrel huddled unhappily in the guttering. It was quickly ringed and released, but a short while later the same bird was fluttering at the glazing again, so this time I brought it into the living room (*Plate 45*). The lure of the light seemed just too strong in the absence of any other landmarks on this dark and overcast night.

STORM PETREL
South Bishop Lighthouse
5th August

"Flutter-walking" - an
unsteady gait, with much
support from its wings.

Sketches made of the individual sitting
on the kitchen table.
winglength: 122 mm
weight: 29.6 gms

(Plate 45)

Once I had made a pot of tea, I took the 'stormie' out of its bag, and sat it on the living room table. This wasn't very much to its liking, so I spread a piece of sack over the formica, to make a better surface for it to walk on. Storm petrels are the smallest of the British seabirds, and many thousands nest on Skokholm and large (but unknown) numbers nest on Skomer. Like the shearwaters they only come to their nest sites after dark, but because they are so tiny they are even more difficult to find. In previous years I had ringed hundreds on Skomer but this was the first opportunity I had to make drawings. As I worked the 'stormie' sat comfortably on the hessian, its little head constantly moving as it looked around the room. About five minutes of inspecting the room seemed sufficient, so it stood up shook its feathers, then walked shakily across the table on long fragile legs. It walked like an old man recovering from a hip operation, not at all confident that his legs would carry him, and occasionally it would open and flutter its wings to help support its weight. It is by this means that the petrel 'walks on water', fluttering and paddling up the wave slopes even in the foulest of weather, to feed on macro-plankton and tiny fish. After a couple of circuits of the piece of sack, and a well-earned rest, it 'flutter-walked' across the table towards me, onto my heavy wool sweater and up my chest to my shoulder. After a breather it achieved its goal by 'flutter-walking' up my face and onto the top of my head! I could see my reflection in the window, crowned by a storm petrel, crouched on my hair and looking around the room rather puzzled. A couple of minutes went by until suddenly it took off and flew out of the living room, through the kitchen and crash-landed on the window-sill of the radio room, where I quickly recaptured it and put it back in a cloth bag, to prevent it sustaining injury. I was captivated by this show of indifference to the human race, but logic told me that the 'stormie' had been looking for the highest point around the table from which to launch itself, which happened to be the top of my head. Most seabirds with long wings and short legs nest on rocky slopes, so that they can gain airspeed by a leap into space from a precipice. It is rather reassuring to be considered on a par with a rock by a tiny bird! I released this tiny sea-elf at dawn and watched till it was out of sight, flying steadily south-west towards the vast Atlantic.

AUGUST 6th   I found a dead swift in the yard below the tower, a youngster with white face and feather tips, so I added some drawings of it to the sheet of adult studies made earlier in the month (*Plate 38*).

AUGUST 7th   Tony called me early for morning watch, at 3.00 a.m., because the overcast squally weather had brought a big attraction of small birds to the light. He had done sterling service and had piled up the dead by the engine room and had a box full of warblers in the store. The beams of the light held dozens of tiny flickering shapes, but the attraction was already waning as the rain passed and visibility improved. I caught a couple of sedge warblers and a willow warbler before it petered out altogether, and found another storm petrel crouched in the gallery guttering! By daybreak I was ready to go through the live ones, ringing, weighing and measuring them before release. The storm petrel went first, off to the south-west just like the first one, and then a total of eight sedge warblers and two willow warblers. Most of these spent the day feeding among the scurvy-grass below the winch gantry and left the following night. There were twenty-five dead, one Manx shearwater which had collided with an aerial mast, four willow warblers, three grasshopper warblers and no less than seventeen sedge warblers. The whole attraction lasted about an hour, but I found it impossible to estimate the number of birds involved. Most of the warblers were young birds, heavy with body fat and setting off on the first stage of migration. Not a very auspicious start to a 4,000-mile journey!

At 8.40 a.m. an immature heron came slowly past the rock beating steadily southwards. A different direction to the previous group, but no less puzzling. There are one or two sites on the Pembrokeshire coast where herons nest on the cliffs, but even they move inland to feed. Still, this is the time of year when immature herons disperse from the breeding areas to winter away from home, so perhaps this is the movement reflected in my recent observations.

AUGUST 8th

Relief day dawned with thunderstorms and torrential rain, and mid-morning we received the unwelcome news that the Trinity House helicopter had broken down and wouldn't be available to take us ashore! All through the day we sat around with all our belongings packed, receiving conflicting radio messages about the state of the helicopter, until we had almost decided to unpack and settle down for another night. Eventually a message came through that we were being brought off by the Trinity House tender *Winston Churchill*. Sure enough, she appeared off-station at 5.30 p.m. and we were on board within fifteen minutes, to enjoy a memorable trip back to **Milford Haven via Skokholm lighthouse, in a heavy sea with a leaden sky** and lightning all around. We cruised through a huge flock of shearwaters all feeding avidly on sand eels and the rough sea actually threw several small fish onto the decks. We arrived in port at 9.00 p.m. and by half-past I was home, unlike my companions from the other lights who were all facing long train journeys through the night.

SEPTEMBER 5th

By early September autumn migration is well under way and small parties of terns pass by South Bishop almost every day. The majority are too far out to identify with any great confidence, but most are either common or Arctic terns, rather similar in piumage and consequently lumped together by unsure ornithologists as 'Commic' terns. Coincidental with the tern passage is the migration of Arctic skuas, bold and piratical relations of gulls, which breed on the Scottish islands (*Plate 46*). They get most of their food by harrying the terns and smaller gulls, forcing them to disgorge their catch, so accompanying the migrating terns assures them of a regular food source. They are superb fliers capable of tremendous acceleration and agility and I have yet to see a bird capable of evading their pursuit. There are two colour phases, pale and dark, the majority of the birds passing South Bishop this month being dark phase.

SEPTEMBER 7th

A small arrival of migrants combined with fine weather persuaded me to fix up a mist net in the rocky valley. There were seven or eight wheatears about and two immature redstarts, flicking their chestnut tails from the aerial wires. All of these seemed quite capable of not getting caught, but in the end I did manage to ring one of the redstarts, which had a momentary lapse of concentration.

SEPTEMBER 9th

Overcast with drizzle last night, so that at 2.00 a.m. there was a large attraction to the light. Lots of small passerines were flitting about and I caught several which were asleep on the window sills. A group of whimbrel circled the light calling incessantly and I longed for the chance to catch one. Surprisingly no birds were killed, which I think was due in part to the light winds which enabled the birds to control their approach to the tower. It was over by 4.00 a.m. and I had been too busy catching birds to notice much about the species involved, so that when I started ringing and releasing them at dawn I was surprised to find seven species represented out of a total fourteen birds caught. There were four wheatears, whose wing measure-ments and general rufous colouring suggested they were of the Greenland race (which migrates south through western Britain), and three spotted flycatchers, two chiffchaffs and two goldcrests, these last being the forerunners of the birds which winter in Britain. Singles of willow, sedge and grasshopper warbler made up this mixed bag and they spent most of the day feeding around the island, much to my delight.

SEPTEMBER 10th

No migrants about today, all departed last night. The Air-Sea Rescue helicopter flew out to us and did a few practice landings on our helipad. They brought us a great armful of newspapers and magazines collected from their Mess Room, so we settled down for a prolonged read during the evening.

SEPTEMBER 14th

There has been a steady passage of swallows and martins over the past few days and occasionally odd pied wagtails too, but the change in the wind, round to north-north-west, brought steadily worsening weather with gale force winds and squally rain. This culminated in an astonishingly severe electrical storm last night, during which the aerial mast was struck by lightning, sending yards of wire crashing in a tangled mass into the yard. The alarm bells brought all three of us out to switch off the beacon and clear up the mess and while we were doing this the mast was struck a second time with a blinding blue flash and stunning bang. The air seemed alive with static and we got small shocks from door handles and railings. The rain was still lashing down so we quickly finished the job and went inside, watching the storm pass over from the relative safety of the living room.

SEPTEMBER 17th

An immature male peregrine was sitting on the wall when I went out to do the 9.00 a.m. weather this morning, resplendent in his rich brown plumage (*Plate 47*). I thought he would fly away when he saw me, but he only moved about twenty yards to an outcrop of rock overlooking the helipad where he sat for about ten minutes, while I made some sketches. He seemed quite content, sitting with his feathers fluffed out, enjoying the sun. Eventually he took off, and circled the island lazily, throwing the gulls and oystercatchers into hysterics, but not really bothering about them. At this point a small bird, which proved to be a linnet, came flying in from the general direction of Ireland. The peregrine decided that a bit of linnet-baiting would be fun, and proceeded to make mock attacks on the, by now, frantically flapping finch. I am sure that the peregrine could have killed it quite easily, but instead he followed the unfortunate bird right across Ramsey Sound, until both were lost from sight. What happened to the linnet afterwards is anybody's guess.

SEPTEMBER 20th

A fine-looking pale-phase Arctic skua came in close under the boat landing to chase some kittiwakes feeding there this morning and gave me excellent views of its aerial prowess, but before long it drifted away southwards, leaving the small gulls to feed in peace.

SEPTEMBER 25th

Several groups of 'Commic' terns went south during a gale, among them was a larger, immature Sandwich tern, beating steadily after its smaller companions.

Skua passage is at its height off Pembrokeshire
in September, with both light phase and dark phase
birds passing by daily. Surprisingly few birds seem
to be in the barred immature plumage, only one so
far. Kittiwakes bear the brunt of the Skua's parasitic
habits, particularly immatures.

Immature
Kittiwake

Dark phase
Arctic Skua

Immature
Arctic Skua

Light phase
Arctic Skua

(Plate 46)

PEREGRINE FALCON
Immature plumage
probably ♂
17th September

This peregrine stayed
around the rocks for
about twenty minutes –
long enough to make
sketches and fill the rest
in from memory.

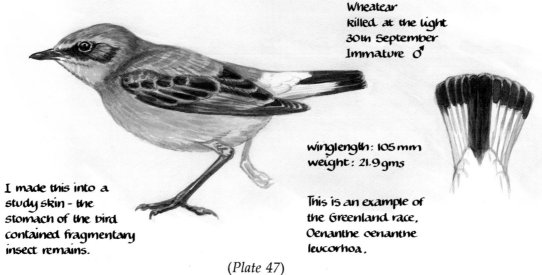

Wheatear
killed at the light
30th September
Immature ♂

winglength: 105 mm
weight: 21.9 gms

I made this into a
study skin – the
stomach of the bird
contained fragmentary
insect remains.

This is an example of
the Greenland race,
Oenanthe oenanthe
leucorhoa.

(Plate 47)

SEPTEMBER 26th   The Arctic skua's larger and more aggressive cousin came by. It was just after 8.00 a.m. that I saw a great skua coming through Ramsey Sound, to pass South Bishop and continue on towards Grassholm. Most seabird watchers (myself included) prefer the Shetland name of Bonxie for this bird, for much of the British breeding population nests in those islands and the name suggests the character of the birds rather well. This one did not chase any other birds while I watched it, but seemed very purposeful in its southward flight.

SEPTEMBER 29th   Ten days ago I caught a fleeting glimpse of a small bird which I thought might be a red-breasted flycatcher, a rarity indeed on the west coast, but it was gone in a flash and the persistent foul weather since the 19th has made prolonged observations on small migrants virtually impossible. This morning the wind had dropped to force four or five and it stopped raining briefly, so that I could get out for a look around. A lot of swallows were moving south, over a hundred this morning, and also three house martins. There were four wheatears around the rocks, but what caught my eye was a group of small birds among the scurvy-grass on the sheltered side of the rock. A wren and a goldcrest certainly, and unmistakably a red-breasted flycatcher! (*Plate 48*) Whether it's the same individual as ten days ago I don't know but it is real enough. I watched it feeding and chivvying the wren, and made some drawings, then fell to thinking how best to catch it. Although it was sheltered here it was really too windy to use a mist net, but in the absence of anything else I had to try. I put up the net below the gantry, and before long the tiny bird was feeding close by, but it could see the net and kept perching on the shelf strings, or flying under it. The wind was steadily increasing and I grew more and more frantic, until I had the little devil perched right in front of the net. A wave of hand and it was in, lying on its back amid the billowing folds. I struggled gleefully down the rocks, opened the net to grasp my prize, and it slipped neatly through the meshes and flew off with a 'chik' of triumph, leaving me disconsolate. As it was spitting with rain again, I packed up the net and left the bird to fly-catch in peace.

SEPTEMBER 30th   I found a dead wheatear this morning, lying below the aerial mast. It was an immature male, and plainly of the Greenland race. I could not decide how it had died, but it had a broken leg and bruised wing and could well have been the crippled individual which had been around for some time, but had evaded my attempts to capture it.

Relief day. While we were waiting for the helicopter a flock of brambling, OCTOBER 3rd
over twenty altogether, passed us going west. A group of Scandinavian
migrants, fleeing west to escape the continental winter, the first of many
more to come.

We arrived on station during a squally rainshower, but it was immediately OCTOBER 31st
apparent that there were quite a few birds about. By the time I got out for a
look around the rain had stopped and a group of small birds were feeding
avidly among the dead scurvy-grass below the living room (*Plates 49 and 50*).
To my surprise this flock contained four snow buntings, three black
redstarts and two skylarks! I quickly put up a small mist net in the most
sheltered site and during the afternoon caught both skylarks, one black
redstart and a snow bunting, these last two were the first of their kind I had
ever ringed. There were a couple of wrens in the rocky valley, and a few
blackbirds, redwings and song thrushes flitting about, some of which had
broken wings, almost certainly the result of collisions with aerial wires. A
search of the rocks produced forty-two dead birds from the previous couple
of nights, including two dozen redwing, fourteen blackbirds, two skylarks
and single starling and song thrush. This must be a reflection of the level of
passage on recent nights and the most dangerous period, around the new
moon, is still a couple of days away.

Two of the three original black redstarts are still with us, but over the past NOVEMBER 5th
few days rather fewer birds have been around; most of the cripples seemed
to have succumbed to the cold and occasional rain. An immature peregrine
circled the rock briefly this afternoon, but soon made off in the direction of
the North Bishop. Towards evening I found a song thrush by the winch
house, its left wing badly smashed. It was very weak and with the limited
resources at my disposal I regretfully decided that the best course of action
was to end its suffering as quickly as possible. I left the little corpse on the
cliff edge, but before I reached the top of the steps a herring gull had
snatched it away. In this harsh environment nothing is ever wasted.

The cawing of rooks and jackdaws is not a sound I had expected to hear NOVEMBER 6th
on South Bishop, but this morning a large mixed flock of about 350 all
told passed over moving north-west, all in good voice. Some of them

REDBREASTED FLYCATCHER
South Bishop
29th September

Very bold and unafraid,
flycatching among dead stems
and occasionally feeding from
perch onto ground like a small
chat.
Evaded all attempts at capture.

Buff spots on the
greater coverts
age this one as
an immature.

The opportunity to make
sketches of a relatively
uncommon bird come only
infrequently. I didn't make
the fullest use of the time
because of my attempts to
catch the little gem. These
few are compiled from the
best of those frantic scribbles.

This Wren was feeding
alongside the Flycatcher,
and suffered constant
chivvying and harassment.

(Note: these sketches not to same scale.)

(Plate 48)

seemed a little undecided about this trip to Ireland, for they kept breaking away from the main flock and circling back towards the mainland with a renewed outbreak of 'chacks' and 'caws'. Eventually the majority decision ruled and I watched them on their north-westerly heading till they were out of sight. Little groups of starlings and greenfinches were also hurrying past, the whole movement seeming to be inspired by the changing winds associated with a passing high pressure system. By early afternoon visible migration had petered out but we shall see what tomorrow brings.

NOVEMBER 7th

The wind moved round to the north-north-east during the night as the high pressure system passed over, so the visible migration this morning was slightly different. A flock of 150 woodpigeons went north-west mid-morning, followed by a couple of skylarks, but the rooks, jackdaws and starlings were coming in off the sea and heading eastwards! There were only about forty rooks and daws and perhaps twenty starlings, but this conflicting movement has me rather puzzled.

NOVEMBER 8th

The continuing passage of the high pressure system brought the winds round to the east this morning, and there they stayed, steadily strengthening till late evening. It was a bright, cold day and the visible migration was virtually constant from early morning till late afternoon. Every few minutes another small group of passerines passed the lighthouse hurrying east towards the mainland, as if a fearsome monster lurked just below the western horizon. Starlings, of course, were obvious, tight little groups passing confidently by. A long procession of rooks and jackdaws was strung from horizon to horizon all day, little groups flapping purposefully by 'cawing' to each other. The puzzling counter-movement of the other day was repeated, 700 jackdaws passing east, over 100 passing west. Over 110 rooks going to Wales, 30-odd heading for Ireland. The paradox was even more noticeable as the day wore on, for I counted thirteen species taking part in the migration, but only the rooks and daws showed any indecision about which way to go. Could it be that when some of them reached the Welsh coast they turned back to pass the information on to those following? If that is the case, then some individuals undoubtedly were counted twice! The little bands of finches were more direct in their flight and more difficult to identify. More than a hundred moved east in a few hours, but only about fifty were identified, the bulk being chaffinches and greenfinches, also a pair of snow buntings and a single male brambling. None of these stopped on the rock, or even deviated from their course towards us but I did see a tiny bird coming in low over the waves, making tough work of heading into

BLACK REDSTART AND SNOW BUNTINGS
South Bishop
31st October

♂

The Black Redstarts ranged freely over the rocks, and were not the least bit shy of coming right in amongst the buildings.

Strange to see these two species side by side, with one nice adult ♂ of each.

The buntings kept very close to the coarse grasses in the gully below the living-room.

♂

(Plate 49)

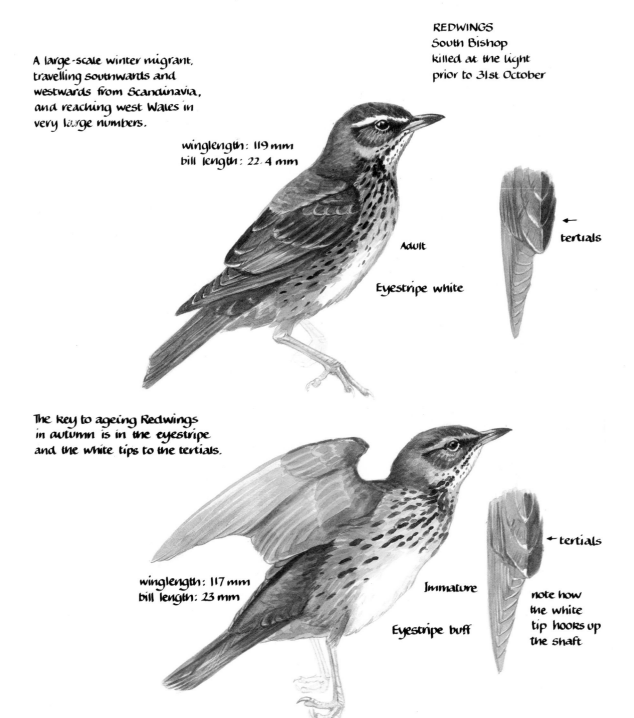

A large-scale winter migrant, travelling southwards and westwards from Scandinavia, and reaching west Wales in very large numbers.

REDWINGS
South Bishop
killed at the light
prior to 31st October

winglength: 119 mm
bill length: 22.4 mm

Adult

Eyestripe white

← tertials

The key to ageing Redwings in autumn is in the eyestripe and the white tips to the tertials.

winglength: 117 mm
bill length: 23 mm

Immature

Eyestripe buff

← tertials

note how the white tip hooks up the shaft

Birds of the Iceland race apparently show very heavy streaking on the underparts. I have yet to find a convincing example!

(Plate 50)

RAVENS
South Bishop
November

Ink and wash drawings
made over the week
following the worst
attraction, when these
birds were daily visitors.

(Plate 51)

the wind. It seemed to take ages to cover the last few yards and I felt sure it would be lost in the breaking waves, but it came steadily on flitting up the rocks to perch on a sheltered patch of scurvy-grass a few yards from my seat. A chiffchaff, paler and greyer than the early autumn birds, probably one of the northern or eastern races. Before I even made a sketch, it flitted away, through the yard and out across the sea towards the mainland, four miles away.

A couple of redwings and blackbirds passed over calling, they are more frequent night migrants and it made me wonder about the extent of this movement. Was it just localised on this narrow stretch of the coast, or more widespread across the Irish Sea? The best, or most unexpected, bird of the day saved its appearance till mid-afternoon, when the bulk of the movement was over. I was standing at the southern edge of the yard when I heard the unmistakable chattering of a magpie, and just saw it perched on top of the winch gantry before it took off and made for the mainland. It is only a couple of hundred years since magpies colonised Ireland from Britain. This one was obviously repaying the compliment, or had come in search of its roots!

Joe, the temporary assistant keeper, woke me at 2.00 a.m. with the news that '. . . there's a lot of birds about!' I was up and dressed in an instant, and grabbing a torch and a handful of bird bags, went into the yard. It was drizzling slightly, misty but calm – the conditions that meant the light would be very attractive to birds unable to navigate by using the moon and stars or familiar landmarks. Joe's understatement floored me. The place was alive with birds, thousands of them, perched on every available wire and ledge, hopping around the yard, and crashing into the glazing. The sky was a blizzard of fluttering shapes, brilliantly illuminated by beams of light and the calls and snatches of song made it difficult to hear. A great band of starlings had taken over the beacon aerial and it sagged under their weight, so that new birds joining at the ends of the cable slid down to the tight knot in the middle, forcing the birds already there to fly out to the edges in a never-ending circle. The gutters and roof tops were thick with starlings, all singing and waving their wings wildly, while redwings were everywhere I looked. Every few seconds I could hear the thump of a bird hitting the glazing and falling into the yard, so I set about catching as many as possible. The floodlights seemed to cause the birds great distress, forcing them up into the deadly merry-go-round of birds caught in the beams. They were there to illuminate the tower, in the belief that this made it easier for birds to avoid collision, but now they were more of a liability. I turned them off, but this made little difference, the thrushes in particular still crashed frantically into every obstacle. Eventually, I hit on the idea of switching off the yard

NOVEMBER 9th

WOODCOCK ♀
Scolopax rusticola
South Bishop
9th November

position
of ear

Killed at the light
during the severe
attraction.
In fine condition,
extremely fat.

head viewed from behind
(eyes in the back of its head!)

winglength: 202 mm
bill length: 70.5 mm

Woodcock are highly nocturnal,
feeding in soft ground, probing
with long sensitive bill.
They have superb night vision,
through almost 360°, and good
hearing, although their ears are
in an odd position.

(Plate 52)

WATER RAIL
Rallus aquaticus
9th November

Immature
Note white throat
and dark eye.

Both these, and another
immature, killed at the light.

Adult ♂
winglength: 121 mm
bill length: 40 mm

FIELDFARE   Adult ♀
Turdus pilaris
9th November
Killed at the light.

winglength: 149 mm
bill length: 24.4 mm
weight: 106 gms

The largest of our British thrushes,
and another Scandinavian visitor
driven south west by the northern
winter.

(Plate 53)

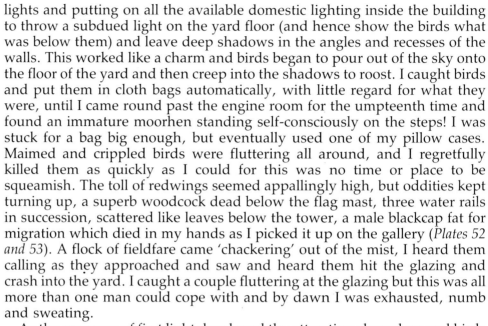

lights and putting on all the available domestic lighting inside the building to throw a subdued light on the yard floor (and hence show the birds what was below them) and leave deep shadows in the angles and recesses of the walls. This worked like a charm and birds began to pour out of the sky onto the floor of the yard and then creep into the shadows to roost. I caught birds and put them in cloth bags automatically, with little regard for what they were, until I came round past the engine room for the umpteenth time and found an immature moorhen standing self-consciously on the steps! I was stuck for a bag big enough, but eventually used one of my pillow cases. Maimed and crippled birds were fluttering all around, and I regretfully killed them as quickly as I could for this was no time or place to be squeamish. The toll of redwings seemed appallingly high, but oddities kept turning up, a superb woodcock dead below the flag mast, three water rails in succession, scattered like leaves below the tower, a male blackcap fat for migration which died in my hands as I picked it up on the gallery (*Plates 52 and 53*). A flock of fieldfare came 'chackering' out of the mist, I heard them calling as they approached and saw and heard them hit the glazing and crash into the yard. I caught a couple fluttering at the glazing but this was all more than one man could cope with and by dawn I was exhausted, numb and sweating.

As the greyness of first light developed the attraction slowed up and birds stopped coming to the light. I gathered the corpses into one pile so that I could go through them later and went over to the shed to start ringing the living. There is a substantial gap at the bottom of the shed door and as I approached a brown shape darted through. When I opened the door, a superb adult snipe was standing under the work bench! (*Plate 54*) Completely unharmed, it was the first to be ringed and released as daylight came. I had caught fifty-five birds, of these, three seemed to be a little concussed, so I let them go unringed, but during the next hour and a half I ringed, weighed and measured and released nineteen redwing, fifteen starlings, twelve blackbirds, two fieldfares and singles of skylark, snipe, moorhen and song thrush (*Plate 55*). The moorhen was particularly interesting for I have rather few historical records of birds from South Bishop, but there is one of a moorhen caught at the light at 1.00 a.m. on 9th October 1884.

After some tea and toast, I set about the task of sorting the casualties. This took some time, as I was careful to check each bird for a ring, but found none. The final tally was pretty depressing; 126 redwing, 67 blackbirds, 10 starlings, 6 fieldfares, 3 water rails, 2 song thrushes, and singles of woodcock, blackcap and skylark. 217 in all, but this was only a fraction of the total night's kill, for when daylight fully came and the mist lifted slightly the sea around the rock was dotted with tiny corpses and the gulls came in from all the outlying islands to feast. In the middle of the morning two ravens also turned up from the mainland and spent the day searching the rocks (*Plate 51*), finding several dead birds I had overlooked. How they knew of the carnage is a mystery to me, for I had not seen them out here before. The corvid passage continued this afternoon, over 750 rooks and 300 jackdaws heading out westwards again, but I was engrossed in making drawings and study skins so I didn't do much other birdwatching.

Yesterday's survivors have largely moved on, but there was another, smaller, attraction last night, which produced eleven birds ringed and ten killed. The most interesting of these were two water rails, the first one unfortunately dead below the tower, but the second captured alive, after a struggle, from among a stack of water hoses. It had crept under the pile when it saw me, and I had the devil of a job to get it out, as it was stuck in the mouth of a hose. Eventually it came out, a bit belligerent and rather dusty, and thanked me for my efforts with a jab in the face from its beak. My reference books say that they are weak fliers but this one hadn't read them and took off like a rocket towards the mainland when I released it at dawn, flying with rapid wader-like wing beats and its long legs trailing. A single raven was back again today, searching carefully among the rocks and no doubt its patience was well rewarded. A change in the weather is forecast, promising southerly winds and more gales combined with the waxing moon, this should bring an end to the death and destruction, for a while at least.

NOVEMBER 10th

The squally weather conditions since the 10th have kept bird movements at a low level and although a few thrushes and starlings have come to the light none has been killed and only about ten caught and ringed. The ravens continue to pay us hopeful visits but they stay a shorter time each day and don't seem to find much. I flushed a woodcock from behind the fuel tanks at midday, and later in the afternoon it was trying to probe for food in the shallow soil below the living room, but without much success. They have large eyes and are well adapted to night flying, so it came as no surprise to see it leave the island at dusk and head towards the mainland.

NOVEMBER 13th

Persistent west to north-west gales have grounded most birds, although there was a movement of starlings at dawn with over 500 passing westwards. Five or six blackbirds are still on the island, and manage to escape the worst of the weather by sheltering in the shallow burrows of the resident pair of rabbits, descendants of a small group brought to the island as pets by a keeper some years ago. The blackbirds seem totally dependent

NOVEMBER 18th

BIRDS IN THE HAND
South Bishop
9th November
Caught at the light
during the severe
attraction

← Snipe
ring number: XA 84424
winglength: 133 mm
weight: 82.5 gms

Skylark ♂ →
ring number: BS 87729
winglength: 111 mm
weight: 38.4 gms

← Starling   Adult ♂
ring number: XA 84438
winglength: 135 mm
weight: 72 gms

(Plate 54)

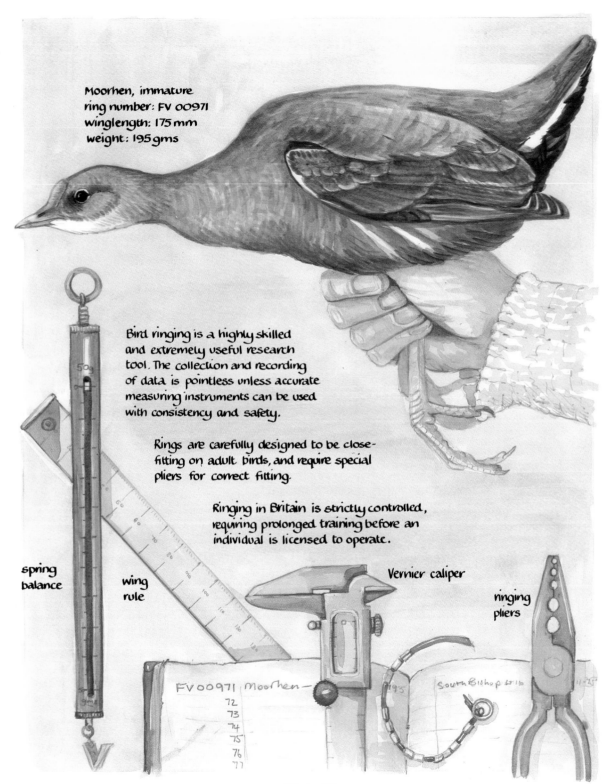

Moorhen, immature
ring number: FV 00971
winglength: 175 mm
weight: 195 gms

Bird ringing is a highly skilled
and extremely useful research
tool. The collection and recording
of data is pointless unless accurate
measuring instruments can be used
with consistency and safety.

Rings are carefully designed to be close-
fitting on adult birds, and require special
pliers for correct fitting.

Ringing in Britain is strictly controlled,
requiring prolonged training before an
individual is licensed to operate.

spring
balance

wing
rule

Vernier caliper

ringing
pliers

FV 00971 Moorhen —

72
73
74
75
76
77

South Bishop Lt Ho

195

(Plate 55)

on our kitchen scraps now, and I think they must all be in a bit of a decline. If they are still around next week when we get nearer to relief day I may try to catch some of them and give them a lift to shore in the helicopter, for they won't survive the winter out here. The fresh-water pool in the rocky valley held a redshank this morning, sheltering from the buffeting wind and driving rain. By afternoon the weather improved slightly and it left us, flying south towards Skomer.

There was an eclipse of the moon tonight, which started at 9.00 p.m. and showed complete cover by 9.20 p.m. The night was clear and bright, making this the best view I have ever had of a lunar eclipse. It had no effect that I could see on any night migrants which may have been around.

NOVEMBER 25th   Back to a period of squally showers, overcast mist and drizzle guaranteed to have a depressing effect on offshore birdwatchers, particularly ones spoiled by the excitement and drama of the early part of the month. The past week has seen little in the way of visible passage, apart from odd groups of starlings or greenfinches on fine days. There have been a few more seabirds passing through, with numbers of kittiwakes and auks moving south and occasionally parties of gannets, mostly adults, going north. Little groups of common scoter have appeared offshore on a couple of mornings, quickly moving southwards in long lines, but on the whole it has become quiet. My plans to capture the blackbirds and take them ashore have suffered a setback, they have all gone, either flown away, or more likely died in the rabbit holes.

During the month I have ringed 79 birds, and recovered 283 dead. How many thousands of migrants actually passed over South Bishop is impossible to estimate.

DECEMBER 29th   We took off from St Ann's Head during a brief lull in the squally showers, the helicopter buffeted by the strong up-currents from the cliffs as we followed the coastline northwards. Basil and I were accompanied by Pete, the new Assistant Keeper assigned to South Bishop from the south coast, where he had seen duty on the Eddystone and Nab Tower. Rough it may have been but we had a grand view of the lines of breakers rolling in from the Atlantic to end their journey pounding the sandstone rocks. As we passed by Skomer we overflew a fine adult peregrine beating steadily towards the island in search of a meal, the flocks of gulls parting at his approach like the Red Sea before Moses! Before too long we arrived on a wet and windswept helipad. Under the onslaught of the weather relief was completed in record time and we spent the rest of the day comfortably ensconced in front of the fire.

The squally showers have persisted throughout the past few days and now the winds are gusting to gale force, lashing the island with drizzle and salt spray. Birds have been very scarce, just a few gulls sheltering in the lee of the rock, and an occasional auk or fulmar flying past, but this afternoon a small group of razorbills was fishing in the boat landing, sheltered from the force of the gale. A dozen or so were diving around the weedy fringes of the rocks, sometimes having to move quickly to avoid being washed onto them by the surging waves. I didn't see them catch anything, but their presence attracted a flock of kittiwakes to flutter and pick at the surface and inevitably a couple of great black-backed gulls brought their own brand of charm, bullying the razorbills mercilessly until the little group dispersed. DECEMBER 31st

A new year and so begins a new bird list! On the mainland I would lay plans to visit as wide a range of habitats as possible to seek out perhaps fifty or sixty species during the day. On South Bishop I sat and waited for birds to appear. Our resident herring gulls started the ball rolling just after dawn, and a steady trickle of kittiwakes moving south into the deteriorating weather were in second place. The resident great black-backs put in an appearance and so the first three species for the year were all gulls. By mid-morning, gulls were all I'd seen but as the wind increased a small passage of auks trickled south, the majority razorbills but with a scattering of guillemots. A single gannet and a couple of shags hurried by during lunch. A prolonged watch from the lantern in the afternoon added only our rock pipits to the day's list of eight species, before the weather broke and gales brought persistent heavy rain which continued until after nightfall. JANUARY 1st

We went to sleep during a gale and woke up to an even worse one. By midday the winds were force ten and if anything getting stronger. Salt spray covered the whole island and waves broke heavily over the helipad and right up to the bottom of the steps. Each time we went out we could taste the salt on our lips. The sea all around was a mass of breakers and foam, right up as far as the North Bishop, while the dull and overcast sky JANUARY 2nd

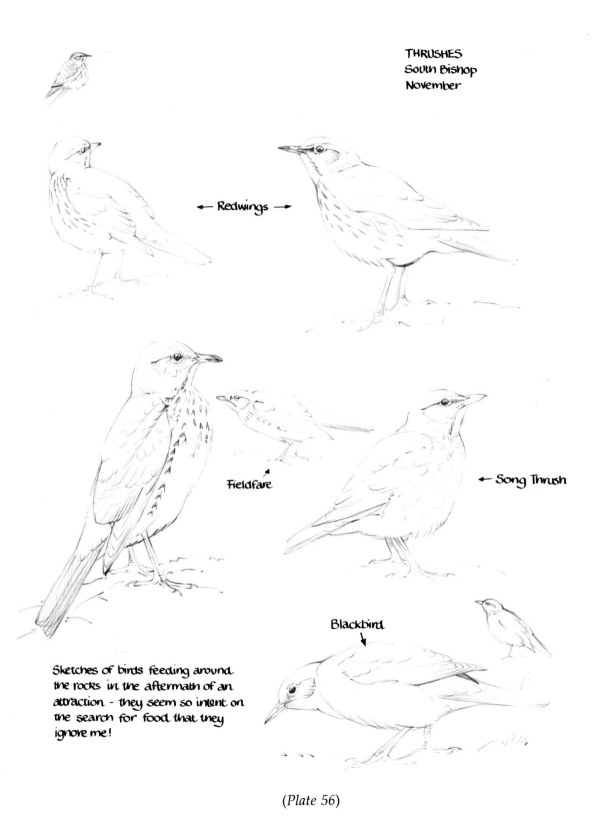

THRUSHES
South Bishop
November

← Redwings →

Fieldfare

← Song Thrush

Blackbird

Sketches of birds feeding around
the rocks in the aftermath of an
attraction - they seem so intent on
the search for food that they
ignore me!

(Plate 56)

periodically closed in even lower over us threatening to turn afternoon into twilight. The 2.00 p.m. gale warning gave indications that things would only get worse, with severe structural damage forecast and, as it was nearing low water, we set out to retrieve all the equipment from the boat landing to prevent it being washed away at high tide. It was uncanny to walk down the rock steps to the landing leaving the howling wind behind, into the relative calm and peace of the sheltered side of the island. As we worked just above the breaking sea we could watch huge rollers thundering past towards Ramsey, diverted by the rock reef to the north and south of us. They seemed to tower above our sheltered rock ledge but their force was directed away from us and we only experienced a steady surging of the water up into the boat landing. At high tide, however, only about six hours away, this place would be repeatedly smashed by many tons of water covering where we stood to a depth of fifteen to twenty feet. As we got back into the lighthouse yard, where conversation was shouted and we were bent double against the force of the wind, a huge roller broke on the rocks, throwing salt spray and foam high over the lighthouse buildings. Suddenly we were standing in a yard running with foam and sea water, soaked to the skin. When the water ran off there was sand and pebbles lying in the yard and I even found seaweed and sand on the gallery floor 160 feet above sea level!

After nightfall the gale became even more ferocious, so that the hourly checks on the generators in the engine room became so potentially dangerous that Pete and I went together for safety. Even so at 10.00 p.m. we could not stand against the force of the wind and had to cross the yard on our hands and knees. It had become simply too hazardous to go outside the main building unnecessarily, so we made a thorough check of the machinery and fuel levels and returned to the safety of the main building, not to venture out again!

JANUARY 3rd

The gale had blown itself out by dawn, and the day was clear and cold, with winds force five to six, westerly. The lighthouse survived the night unscathed, but the amount of sand, shingle and seaweed scattered around the yard was ample proof of the ferocity of the storm. The sea was still very rough though, with a long rolling swell crashing around the rocks stirring up sufficient food to attract twenty or thirty kittiwakes to feed in the tide stream. News reports at midday on the radio proved the extent of the near hurricane, with 80 to 100 miles per hour winds around us in the southern Irish Sea but even stronger winds and extensive damage in a path of destruction right across Wales and England as far as East Anglia! We felt rather proud that South Bishop had borne the worst of the hurricane without even the loss of a slate or tile!

JANUARY 6th   The unsettled squally weather continues although the winds are rather lighter now than a week ago. Birds are still few and far between, and despite adopting a dry viewpoint up in the lantern during the day, I have seen only our resident gulls and rock pipits in any numbers. A couple of redwing passed over during darkness last night, and a single redshank stopped briefly among the rocky pools during a squally shower. It sheltered among the rocks for an hour, but as soon as the rain eased and visibility improved it made off towards the mainland.

JANUARY 7th   Another rough night with gales, but only reaching force eight, mild by recent standards. It is noticeable the extent to which birds have been absent during this prolonged foul weather, very few land birds moving, and even the seabirds apparently giving us a wide berth. I wonder whether they are all farther out to sea, or are they closer inshore feeding around the more sheltered bays and inlets? Our rabbits have been about and this afternoon a seal was eating a large flatfish in the waters of the boat landing (*Plate 57*). We had a brief visit from the Air-Sea Rescue helicopter from Brawdy, they came to make some practice landings on the pad, and kindly brought all the newspapers and magazines from their Mess Rooms, so we spent the evening catching up on world events.

JANUARY 13th   A calm day, but cold, produced a few signs of visible passage in the early morning. Three rooks and a jackdaw passed over westwards and mid-morning five greenfinches in a compact flock stopped briefly on the rock before continuing towards Ramsey.

JANUARY 17th   Continuing calm, though still cold. Very few birds over the past three or four days, although a flock of fifty common scoter flew past us in a long line yesterday, making towards the Smalls Lighthouse. I counted eighteen fine black drakes among them and this is the largest group I have yet seen from South Bishop.

As I was going over to the engine room just before lighting-up time two **porpoises** came past the boat landing, heading north. I hadn't expected to see them here in winter, they always make me think of summer and autumn on this stretch of coast.

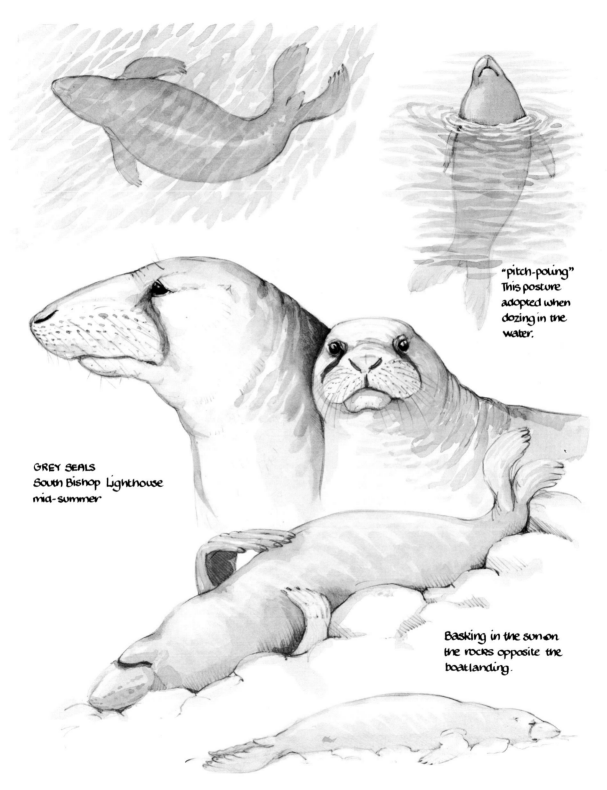

"pitch-poling"
This posture
adopted when
dozing in the
water.

GREY SEALS
South Bishop Lighthouse
mid-summer

Basking in the sun on
the rocks opposite the
boat landing.

(Plate 57)

underwing pattern

LAPWING
South Bishop
21st February

Found dead on the engine-
room roof - had been killed
at the light several days
previously.
Immature, sex not known
winglength: 230 mm
bill length: 24.4 mm

First record for South Bishop

Both these specimens were
rather high, the siskin being
too far gone to be saved.

Siskin   Adult ♂
found in a gutter
21st February
winglength: 72mm
First record for South Bishop

(Plate 58)

CORY'S SHEARWATER
Calonectris diomedea
22nd February
South Bishop

Immature Gannet
showing a similar
pattern and colour scheme.

Fulmar
for comparison

Flew past going SW at 11.00 hrs.
Accepted by British Birds Rarities Committee.
First Pembrokeshire record.

(Plate 59)

JANUARY 23rd   Relief day. There you are, the past week has seen our month end as it began, with solid gales and foul weather for the past six days and no let up on relief day. In fact, had there been much sign of an imminent break in the weather, relief would probably have been postponed. As it was, thanks to the skill of the pilot and flight engineer we came ashore in a force eight gale, although the rain kept off. ·

My month's species total reflected the bad weather, eighteen birds and three mammals!

FEBRUARY 20th   Apart from patchy sea fog and undoubted nip in the air, conditions for relief were very good with only light southerly winds. A little group of six greenfinches was feeding on the rubbish patch and a blackbird and song thrush were all in residence, although I could not see whether they were cripples.

FEBRUARY 21st   Greenfinches were still with us this morning but the blackbird and thrush had gone, so they must have been uninjured after all. Later I was up on the gallery, giving the lantern glazing a good soapy wash when I noticed a dead lapwing lying on the engine-room roof. This was the first record of the species on South Bishop so I decided that after I'd finished I would go up and collect it. In the meantime I continued with my chore, but soon realised that the guttering of the annexe roof was filling up with soapy water, presumably because the down pipe was blocked. It amazes me how doing one chore triggers off several others so I came down from the lantern and brought the ladder to remove the obstruction. Five rather soggy, slightly smelly redwings and a male siskin were jammed in the filter at the top of the down pipe, and when I collected the lapwing it was rather rotten as well. I made a fragile study skin of it but the smaller birds were no good, other than as the source of a reference drawing (*Plate 58*). All had been killed at least a week previously and it is strange that two species, siskin and lapwing, had not been recorded on South Bishop before. It shows how much bird movement goes unnoticed on even a small rock like this one.

FEBRUARY 22nd   A stiff south-westerly wind this morning brought a steady procession of gannets moving out towards Grassholm and from the shelter of the winch-house steps I sat down to look out for an early Manx shearwater. There were a number of fulmars passing by, and at about 11.00 a.m. another one came by followed by a darker bird, which I thought to be a northern 'dark-phase' fulmar. When it came within binocular range I changed my mind, for here was an excellent view of Cory's shearwater, a very rare Atlantic and Mediterranean species, which I knew to be the first record for Pembrokeshire (*Plate 59*). I made a lot of sketches and notes, and it came so close that even its pale bill and white rump patch were easy to see. In the steady breeze its flight was quite un-shearwater-like, with a stiff flapping interspersed by long glides, rather like the fulmars nearby and occasionally an impressive soaring over the wave crests reminiscent of a gannet. In only a few minutes it was lost from sight, moving away to the south-west, and the rest of the seawatch was a bit of an anticlimax. So I spent the afternoon writing up my notes and working up my sketches into more useful reference drawings.

FEBRUARY 26th

The last few nights have seen a steady passage of redwing and thrushes close by the lantern around midnight. Tonight the passage continued, but the weather changed to a thick fog, resulting in an attraction to the light between 1.00 a.m. and 6.00 a.m. Large numbers of redwing, starling and blackbirds, probably over 200, were scattered all around the yard and rocks but mercifully didn't seem to be badly affected by the light and only a blackbird and two redwings were killed. They also proved to be rather more difficult to catch, but I did ring seven redwings, four starlings and two blackbirds. By daylight birds were dotted all over the rock including a dozen fieldfares and four or five pied wagtails. The fog lifted at 7.30 a.m. and our visitors promptly left for the richer feeding grounds on the mainland.

FEBRUARY 27th

The first Manx shearwater of the year passed the light just before midnight, calling raucously, followed a little later by a group of sad-whistling golden plover. About twenty meadow pipits were attracted and I ringed two which were asleep at the base of the tower. When daylight came the island was fairly quiet but a couple of small birds among the dead scurvy-grass caught my eye and I was delighted to find a pair of stonechats feeding avidly (*Plate 60*). The male was quite magnificent, richly rufous on the breast, with deep black and brown upper parts. The female, although dowdy by comparison, was neatly attired in buff and warm brown and no less attractive to look at. They seemed to be strongly attracted to each other and whenever I saw them they were only a yard or two apart at most.

STONECHATS
South Bishop

27th February
This pair, the first Stonechats
recorded on South Bishop, stayed
for a couple of days, finding a
surprising amount of insect prey
among the rocks.

This Song Thrush was killed at the light,
28th February. On closer examination it
showed a sheep-tick firmly attached to
the skin above one eye.

Castor Bean Tick
Ixodes ricinus
Drawn through a
magnifier ×10

(Plate 60)

Another attraction last night, albeit a small one comprising a few redwings, the odd skylark and a lot of meadow pipits. I ringed four pipits and a skylark, but the most interesting find was a sheep tick, attached to the head of a dead song thrush picked up below the tower this morning. I had been asked to look out for these little parasites by a research worker at the School of Veterinary Medicine in Cambridge, so I carefully removed this one and preserved it in a small tube of alcohol. Ticks are fairly common on birds and scientists are interested in the possibility of migrants from Africa bringing tropical ticks, and hence tropical tick-borne diseases, to infect livestock in Europe. So far there has been little concrete evidence, although it is a monumental task likely to take many years to produce results. In due course I received an acknowledgement to my letter which identified the tick as *Ixodes ricinus*, or the Castor Bean tick, probably the commonest species in Britain and therefore unlikely to be of great significance!

FEBRUARY 28th

My efforts to capture the stonechats were finally rewarded today, when I found the male caught in a mist net I had set to catch some of the dozen or so greenfinches around the rock. In the hand he was more magnificent than ever and the way he adopted threat postures at my camera as I took some photographs gave a fair indication of the mood he was in! The female evaded capture (and so did all but one of the greenfinches), but later in the afternoon the pair were feeding together again in the rocky gully.

FEBRUARY 29th

A deterioration in the weather brought cold squally conditions increasing to a southerly gale by mid-afternoon. There was a steady passage of lesser black-backed and common gulls past the rock heading north, and when I went out for a last look around at dusk I found a little trio of birds sheltering in a close huddle among the rocks by the beacon aerial. A woodpigeon, a dunlin and a song thrush were all hunched up in typical sleeping postures in the crevice between the rocks and the lighthouse wall.

MARCH 6th

The gale over the last couple of days seems to have deprived us of our stonechat pair and indeed the calm cold weather which replaced the strong winds has little to recommend it to a birdwatcher. I tried to catch some pollack this morning, but they didn't want to know about limpets or chicken feathers and I gave up after an hour.

We were having a cup of tea at about lunchtime when we heard a propeller-driven aircraft approaching. Jet fighters from Brawdy are fairly common passers-by, but anything with propellers is worth a second look, so

MARCH 8th

we went outside to see a fine old R.A.F. Shackleton circling around us before heading out towards the Smalls Lighthouse. Shackletons were the long-range eyes of Air, Sea Search and Rescue services for many years until they were superseded by the modern Nimrods. Why this one graced us with her presence we shall never know but it made the day more memorable.

MARCH 14th   Squally conditions and gales have kept the THV *Winston Churchill* away for four days, although it did bring an increase in the numbers of shearwaters around the rock. Today the wind decreased to force five to six, and despite a heavy swell the *Churchill* landed a radio engineer on station so that he could sort out the teething problems with our new Side Band set. He will stay on South Bishop until the helicopter relief next week.

MARCH 18th   After a series of quiet days with little to show, this morning produced a few surprises. A male stonechat was perched on the yard wall while we were having breakfast and it was easy to see that he wasn't ringed. It surprises me how often the first record of a species on South Bishop is quickly followed by other individuals. This one stayed around all day but defied my attempts to catch it. Two meadow pipits were not quite so lucky though, for I managed to net them from a scattered group of thirty or so which stopped briefly on their passage eastwards. A few rooks and jackdaws drifted west this morning and a single raven was searching hopefully among the rocks, but without much success. The highlight of the day was undoubtedly the display flight of a pair of peregrines, who twisted and spiralled in the blue sky for at least ten minutes. The male kept making passes and feints at the female and at one point they grappled talons and twisted in a somersaulting spiral, to break free only fifty feet above the sea. It was breathtaking to watch the skill and aerial dexterity of this joint display and on a warm sunny morning it seemed almost made to entertain us. I was a bit disappointed when they drifted away, still spiralling upwards, towards Ramsey.

MARCH 19th   Relief day. Squally overcast with persistent drizzle, our helicopter arrived on station earlier than expected catching us a little bit unawares, but we got away safely at 1.30 p.m. leaving the island in the charge of our companions on the other crew.

Springtime, and the prospect of the peak migration period fills me with   APRIL 16th
anticipation. As our helicopter circled the island, rafts of puffins were
dotted all around on the sea. Later on I watched several of these little groups
interspersing fishing and preening with bouts of vigorous displaying,
circling each other with much head nodding and posturing. It was
noticeable how bright and prominent their bills were even at long range.
There was no sign of migrants around the rock, but that didn't affect my
optimism!

Overcast and misty conditions last night brought a great number of   APRIL 17th
shearwaters to the light, and I succeeded in ringing eleven which crash-
landed in the yard. There were also a few small passerines dotted about and
I caught a goldcrest and a chiffchaff, both of whom were feeding among the
new growth of scurvy-grass this morning. There were eight or nine
wheatears about the rocks too, so I put up a mist net, but only succeeded in
catching one of a pair of linnets which arrived mid-morning. Small numbers
of meadow pipits were passing over, and at one point there were two
wagtails on the rocks below the living room, one a typical British pied and
the other a dazzlingly smart white wagtail, the continental sub-species of
our British bird. These spring white wagtails are often seen in west Wales
and they are presumed to be on their way to Iceland and points north. One
of the delights of spring birdwatching is the immaculate plumage of many of
the adults, and this bird was no exception.

I was surprised to see no less than a dozen seals on the haul-out by the
boat landing at low tide, the highest number I have yet recorded on South
Bishop.

Another attraction last night, but smaller, I caught two shearwaters and a   APRIL 18th
nice wheatear but there were a fair number of small birds about, mostly
either willow warblers or chiffchaffs, and at least two whimbrel circled the
tower just after 11.00 p.m. A couple of willow warblers and chiffchaffs
stayed on today, along with two goldcrests and a wren, but the rock was
generally quiet, undoubtedly due to the increasingly thick mist. I did see a
large flock of common scoter passing by during the morning, I counted over
a hundred before they were lost from sight heading northwards.

A remarkable day, during which the island seemed to be a snack bar on the   APRIL 19th
main road of spring migration, such was the diversity of species stopping
over and passing by. It began with a substantial attraction of willow

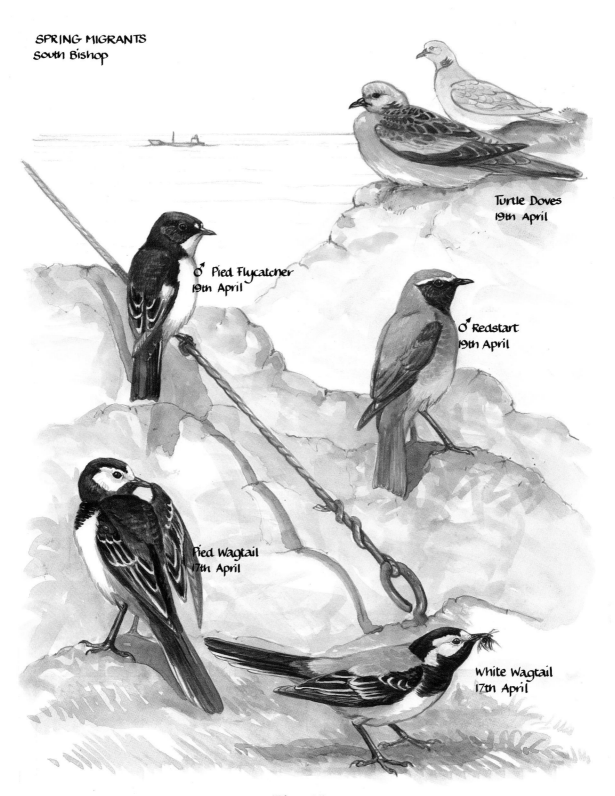

SPRING MIGRANTS
South Bishop

Turtle Doves
19th April

♂ Pied Flycatcher
19th April

♂ Redstart
19th April

Pied Wagtail
17th April

White Wagtail
17th April

(Plate 61)

MERLIN AND WHIMBREL
South Bishop

This female Merlin arrived
during the morning of 22nd
April, and stayed until mid-
afternoon. It killed and ate
at least one Wheatear, before
moving off northwards. Some
spectacular aerial shots.

Whimbrel

27th April
Two Whimbrel were
dozing on the rocks by
the helipad at first light,
but left the island
before midday.

(Plate 62)

warblers and chiffchaffs, dancing and flickering in the mist beams of the lantern. At least fifty of the tiny birds were held by the light for over half an hour, and during this time, I caught seven willows and a single chiffchaff. At one stage a huge shape drifted close to the lantern and then swept away to catch a squealing warbler and devour it in flight. This short-eared owl stayed around the light for an hour and caught several more warblers, but evaded all my attempts to capture it. At first light most of the warblers were down amongst the scurvy-grass, along with a goldcrest and a smart female redstart. I picked up a dozen dead willow warblers and two dead chiffchaffs scattered below the lantern – a couple of these seemed to be the remnants of the owl's meal.

After breakfast I had a more thorough look around and found four or five wheatears and a smart pied flycatcher, resplendent in black and white. A chaffinch, two goldfinches and a redpoll were picking over the rubbish pile, while an odd assortment of wagtails, pipits and linnets stopped briefly before pushing on towards the mainland. In the afternoon I sat on the wall watching the passage and trying to identify some of the participants. Curlew and whimbrel drifted north in pairs, often only located by their calls in the distance, swallows, quick and decisive, in groups of four or five and even a solitary collared dove, in its own eccentric way heading for Ireland while everyone else is hell bent on going north!

APRIL 22nd   The northward trend continues under the influence of light east to north-east winds, and over the past couple of days the warbler numbers have stayed high, with fifteen to twenty around all the time. Once again mostly willow warblers and chiffchaffs, but including the occasional blackcap and sedge warbler (*Plate 62*). A stunningly sooty male black redstart yesterday morning was only excelled by a dashing and predatory female merlin today, who spent the morning chasing wheatears around the rocks and left us in the afternoon, leaving a couple of piles of wheatear feathers to show where she had been. The most unexpected bird of the day, indeed of the month as a whole, was a robin which turned up this morning, stayed for twenty minutes and presumably moved on, although I didn't see it go.

APRIL 28th   Another female merlin today, but this one didn't choose to hunt the wheatears, even though there were over fifty dotted about the island. Many of these seemed to be birds of the Greenland race, judging by the comparison of their size and rich brown colour. So when I managed to catch a couple at the light it was gratifying to note that these two at least fitted the measurements of that race. Two redstarts were much in evidence early this

SMALL MIGRANTS
South Bishop
April

Pied Flycatcher

♂ Redstart

These among several dozen
small birds passing through
during early April.

Sedge Warbler

Small sketches like this
aim to catch the structure
and posture. They are also
a pleasant way to spend
an hour or two!

Spotted Flycatcher

Tree Pipit

Meadow Pipit

(Plate 63)

morning, the male was particularly resplendent in fiery orange, grey and black. They seemed to be mild-mannered birds compared with the pugnacious wheatears, and on more than one occasion I saw a wheatear steal an insect from the female redstart, to which she only put up the most token response (*Plate 63*).

Pipits can be difficult to identify at the best of times, so when I came across two feeding together on the mass of rock sea-spurry by the winch house, I assumed them to be meadow pipits, until they flew to the other side of the rock, uttering the thin high call so typical of tree pipits! Subsequently I noted several others passing over the rocks, often located by their distinctive call note. These are very much summer visitors and so their appearance now is not altogether unexpected.

APRIL 29th   Quite suddenly, a change in the weather, to a cold, cloudy and generally less pleasant day, although the winds remain light. Very few birds of any note throughout the day, so I busied myself with sketches and notes, until late in the evening when Pete called me to look at something outside. He had seen what he took to be a cat sitting on a rock, silhouetted against the setting sun, so we went down to the helipad to look for it. Sure enough the upright shape was sitting there, complete with prominent ears, but closer examination produced a long-eared owl, somewhat indignant at being the centre of attention (*Plate 64*). After a few minutes it moved to a new perch on the rocks below the engine room, before taking wing and floating softly away. I was amazed to see both long-eared and short-eared owls here within ten days of each other, particularly as the long-eared is a shy and unobtrusive night migrant, seldom seen in west Wales. Out here its bark-patterned plumage was little help, and we had probably the best views ever of a wild long-eared.

APRIL 30th   The cold continues, and apart from a few swallows and house martins the visible passage has come to a halt. This evening I sat on the rock steps overlooking the helipad, watching the comings and goings of the Manx shearwaters offshore, when I noticed a slight movement amongst the scurvy-grass growing near my foot. I sat very still, and over the next couple of minutes the tremors came again, until a bright eye and thin bill peered at me from among the leaves, soon to reveal itself as a grasshopper warbler. For the next couple of minutes it fed quietly around the scurvy-grass, occasionally coming out to perch on my boot, which it took to be a rock, before making another sortie after insects. Pete turned up during one of these periods when the tiny bird was amongst the foliage, and he sat down

LONG-EARED OWL
South Bishop
29th April

Arrived on the rock a little before dusk,
and only stayed for a few minutes before
heading east towards the mainland with
determined wing beats.
Its flight over water seemed more positive
and less ponderous than the Short-eared Owl.
Surprisingly cat-like when sitting on the
rocks, bark-pattern camouflage doesn't work
on a rocky island!

(Plate 64)

beside me, asking what I was watching. I didn't say, but told him to sit quietly and watch the scurvy-grass. In a short while the grasshopper warbler popped up again, and Pete was captivated by its tameness. He asked where it had come from and on being told that it was a migrant newly arrived from Africa, he was suitably impressed, so much so that over the next few days he became increasingly absorbed and eventually hooked as a birdwatcher.

MAY 6th   Misty conditions brought an upsurge in the numbers of migrants after the brief lull caused by the change in the weather. Good numbers of sedge and willow warblers were attracted, and about a dozen ringed, along with grasshopper warblers, blackcaps, the odd wheatear and a few shearwaters. Waders have been prominent during these misty nights with dunlin, whimbrel, ringed plover and common sandpiper calling around the light, while purple. sandpipers and turnstones feed on the tideline by day. A couple of porpoises were feeding in the tide stream this evening, attracting gannets and kittiwakes to investigate. Several of the gannets dived and caught mackerel quite close in, so I had a try with my fishing rod and mackerel-feathers from the boat landing, but caught nothing. I was then shown how to fish properly by the professionals when a cow seal which had been watching me from the rocks slid elegantly into the water, dived and re-appeared a couple of minutes later with a small skate, which it proceeded to eat right in front of me. I took the hint, packed up my gear and had beans on toast for tea!

MAY 7th   Sea mist last night produced a large attraction in the early hours, small warblers were everywhere, the sky full of flickering white shapes held in the beams. Most of these small birds look rather similar in the dark, so I didn't have too much idea of the species involved until daylight came and I could look around the rocks. Of one unfortunate casualty I could be sure, however, for as I tried to catch a sedge warbler which was fluttering at the glazing a woodpigeon hit the lantern guttering and died instantly, leaving great drifts of grey and white feathers all over the yard. It brought home to me how dangerous a place the gallery could be during an attraction, for had the pigeon hit me the result could have been a serious fall.

At daybreak I went through the bags, ringing and releasing the night's captures. Fifteen sedge warblers, ten willow warblers, four whitethroats, two grasshopper warblers and a shearwater. One bag held a willow warbler with a ring already on it which needed checking to see if it was one of mine. In the event the ring, 836313, was a stranger and so I sent the details to the

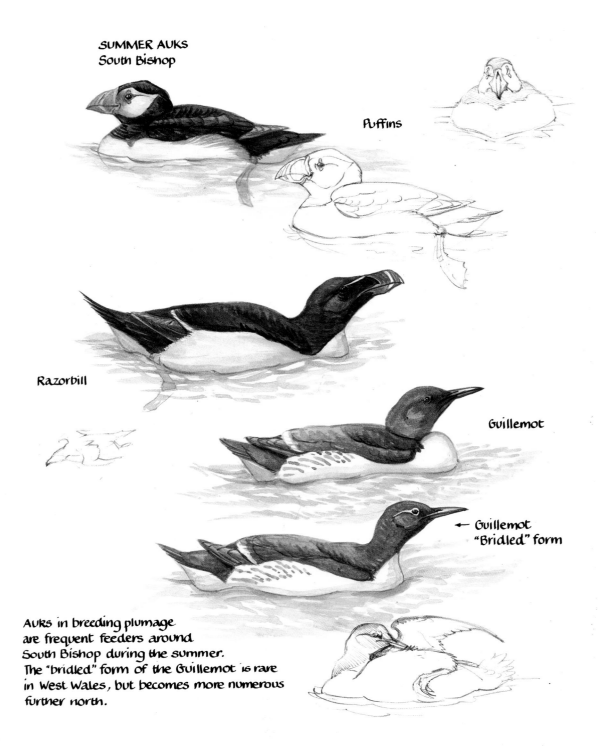

SUMMER AUKS
South Bishop

Puffins

Razorbill

Guillemot

← Guillemot
"Bridled" form

Auks in breeding plumage
are frequent feeders around
South Bishop during the summer.
The "bridled" form of the Guillemot is rare
in West Wales, but becomes more numerous
further north.

(Plate 65)

Ringing Office at the British Trust for Ornithology, and in due course received notification that it had been ringed two days previously (on the 5th May), on Lundy Island off the north coast of Devon, ninety kilometres south-east.

In daylight the extent of the arrival was plain to see, sedge and willow warblers were everywhere, probably over 150 in number, and also lots of whitethroat, grasshopper warblers, goldcrests, chiffchaffs, wheatears and redstarts. The island was alive with bird song as the night migrants searched every crevice for insects. There was plenty of movement overhead too, for swallows and martins were passing continually. In the afternoon THV *Winston Churchill* landed oil and water on station and from my position in the winch house I had a grand view across the Sound towards Ramsey, where I could see little flocks of pipits and occasional wagtails on the move. A flock of twenty-six collared doves came by, the most I have seen together from South Bishop, once again all heading for Ireland. As dusk fell the weather improved, the clouds clearing to reveal a starlit sky, just the conditions night migrants would need to leave South Bishop and complete their interrupted journeys.

MAY 8th   Sure enough, a clear starlit night resulted in virtually all our migrants disappearing as suddenly as they came. The few odd willow warblers and wheatears remaining are probably injured. The weather is forecast to deteriorate, with fog at first and squally showers developing, weather guaranteed to slow down spring migration to a trickle.

MAY 14th   Relief day. The past week has been a mix of fog and sun and showers, but little in the way of migrants other than swallows and martins. There is almost no vegetation on South Bishop to show the effects of spring, but as we flew by Skomer on the trip home the whole island was purple and mauve with a haze of bluebells. On the outward trip, it had been a dull olive green.

JUNE 11th   We arrived on station during a brief shower, but it was plain to see that there were no migrants present, and only small numbers of seabirds around. This is the height of the breeding season, and the attention of our regular gulls and auks is fully taken up providing for their offspring, so I expect this to be a quiet month and with any luck the weather will give us plenty of opportunity for fishing and lying in the sun!

So much for the sun! From dawn to just after midday we had thick fog, the afternoon overcast and hazy. Visibility was down to less than half a mile and we were sounding the fog signal for about eight hours. I found an oystercatcher's nest containing two eggs this afternoon, situated on a ledge only twenty feet from one fog signal emitter! One of the pair was sitting this evening, its mate standing guard on the helipad, occasionally flying up to chase a herring gull.

The overcast conditions continued through the night and on into today, until by 2.30 p.m. it became necessary to sound for fog once again. There was a single turtle dove (*Plate 61*) on the rock this evening and the rabbits have a single baby, still rather small. The little family were feeding on kitchen scraps below the yard wall when Basil and I went down to the boat landing to try for some fish. We flogged away for an hour or so, but only raised three pollack, one of Basil's pair being a nice fish of nearly two pounds. He filleted them out and put some in the freezer, but I didn't join him in a fish supper, it isn't one of my favourite foods!

The fog cleared this morning, and we were able to turn off the fog signal after over ninety hours continuous sounding! I have never known fog to persist for nearly four days but the light winds and high humidity have kept us bottled up in an oppressive world of swirling shapes and clammy condensation and we were very relieved to be out of it. Nothing cuts you off from the outside world quite so much as a dense fogbank, for it obscures the vision and distorts sound to an incredible degree. More than once in the past few days I have thought I heard a ship making for us on a collision course, only to have it pass safely by beyond the range of vision. Living with a fog signal is strange too. The compressors and their engines need constant care and attention, frequent rests and extra fuel, so they are visited every hour but outside the main building ear defenders are essential, so they are worn permanently around the neck. The diaphone fog signal here gives three deep resonating blasts in a group, at intervals of forty-five seconds, and is audible under normal conditions up to ten miles away. Stand next to the engine room when it is operating, (wearing ear-defenders of course!) and you can feel the ground vibrate. After a period of time, however, the noise becomes part of everyday life, until you hardly hear it and in fact only register it subconsciously, so that on many occasions you think that it has stopped and become increasingly panic-stricken, until, when you are on the point of rushing out to see to it, the blessed thing roars again in mockery!

OYSTERCATCHER - South Bishop

Adult mobbing a Herring Gull

Brown juvenile plumage

Adult (probably ♀) with one of the chicks 20th June

(Plate 66)

♂ Whinchat
2nd July

Mirage over Grassholm
28th June

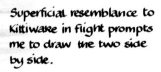

Little Gull
Larus minitus
Immature
Sitting on the rocks with
Kittiwakes in the afternoon.

Superficial resemblance to
Kittiwake in flight prompts
me to draw the two side
by side.

(Plate 67)

JUNE 19th   Our three rabbits are still around most evenings and there seems to be a good flush of fresh growth for them, with plenty of scurvy-grass about, itself a good source of vitamin C, although I prefer the taste of oranges! A couple of porpoises were sporting in the boat landing at high tide, but they didn't stay long. I thought I saw them again later, but it may have been another pair.

JUNE 20th   We've had a happy event! This morning the resident oystercatcher pair were very agitated, calling vociferously and mobbing the local gulls if they so much as blinked in their direction. I hadn't been to the nest site for a couple of days, for fear of disturbing the female, so I concluded that her eggs had hatched in the meantime. Sure enough after about twenty minutes I spotted two chicks, following their parents uncertainly around the helipad (*Plate 66*). While I watched a herring gull swooped low over the little family, and seemed to take a swipe at one of the youngsters. The parents reacted immediately, one bird calling the chicks to it, while the other took wing and mobbed the gull with surprising ferocity, chasing it well out over the sea before returning to its mate, and indulging in a greeting ceremony with more than a hint of triumph in it! When I went down to ring the chicks they all reacted differently however. The young ran off into the broken rocks and crouched, relying on their camouflage to evade me, while the parents called loudly from the rocks. It took only a minute to fit the rings and the parents were soon back fussing around and leading their offspring down to the weedy fringes of the tidal rockpools.

I went to bed for a couple of hours after my morning watch, but woke up at about 3.00 p.m. to the sound of unfamiliar footsteps on the landing. It was misty and damp outside, with patches of sea fog. There were wet footprints through the landing, and I caught a glimpse of a shadowy figure in black walking through the yard. For one awful moment I imagined that we had been captured by some hostile commando force, so was much relieved to find about a dozen wet-suited men drinking tea with Basil and Pete in the living room. The yard was full of equipment and water-proofs and the boat landing held a flotilla of canoes. Our visitors turned out to be an intrepid band of canoeists from the Army Outward-Bound Centre at Tywyn. They had canoed down the Welsh coast and out to South Bishop, a distance of about eighty miles, to get in training for a forthcoming Army expedition to Elephant Island in Antarctica. They had arranged a rendezvous with their pick-up vehicles on Whitesands Bay, practically the nearest mainland beach to South Bishop, only four or five miles away, so they were able to stay with us until early evening, when we watched them until they were out of sight in the patchy sea mist.

The weather continues hot and dry, temperatures of over eighty degrees JUNE 25th
Fahrenheit during the day, seldom dropping below seventy degrees at
night. We have been forced to restrict our use of fresh water to cooking and
limited washing. There is no dramatic shortage here but it is prudent to save
water wherever we can. To this end we cut the top out of a forty-gallon oil
drum, fitted a couple of rope strops and lowered it into the sea on our
winch. This great drum of seawater standing on the gantry provides all we
need to flush the lavatory, provided we carry it in a bucket!

Today also produced some visible migration, but not of birds! While I was
watching from the cliff top looking towards Skomer Island there was a
steady procession of butterflies heading out to sea! Most of them were
identifed as either 'brown ones' or 'white ones', but a few were unmistake-
ably large whites, red admirals and painted ladies. Not many of these
actually came to the rock, but this evening I was sitting on the wall drinking
tea when I noticed a small creature hovering over the low vegetation,
visiting the tiny mauve flowers of rock-spurry. It looked for all the world
like a humming bird, but was a hummingbird hawk moth, the first I had
ever seen in west Wales. This one stayed around for ten minutes from about
9.30 p.m. and then vanished without a trace.

The very hot weather continues, daytime temperatures pushing up to JUNE 28th
eighty-eight degrees Fahrenheit today. A strange phenomenon has been the
very small decrease in temperature at night, only a few degrees at most,
which makes sleeping difficult and creates an oppressive atmosphere. There
has been sea haze for most of the past few weeks, indeed it is closely
associated with very hot weather, but this afternoon I saw what I took to be
a mirage for the first time. I was watching the steady passage of swifts
southwards, when I happened to look at Grassholm Island which lies on the
horizon about seven or eight miles away. Instead of the familiar dark hump
frosted with the white of a gannet colony I could see a flat-topped structure
with towering columnar sides, looking for all the world like a tabular iceberg
(*Plate 67*). It didn't seem any less solid or imposing through binoculars, and
as it didn't show any signs of disappearing I brought my telescope and
tripod and had a good look at it at forty times magnification. I could then
make out the recognisable summit of Grassholm, and one of its offshore
rocks, but the remainder of the mirage seemed as solid and ice-like as ever.
It was quite unsettling, looking at a seemingly solid object which I knew was
not there! I didn't see it go, but about fifteen minutes later Grassholm was
back to normal, and very re-assuring too.

A small group of guillemots came ashore while Pete and I were fishing
this afternoon and we managed to cut one off from its companions and
catch it, but not without getting bitten. Although it has an acutely pointed

GUILLEMOT
South Bishop
27th June

Caught by Pete and me,
and ringed - number GK 09781.

These sketches made while the
bird wandered around the yard.

very penguin-like!

(Plate 68)

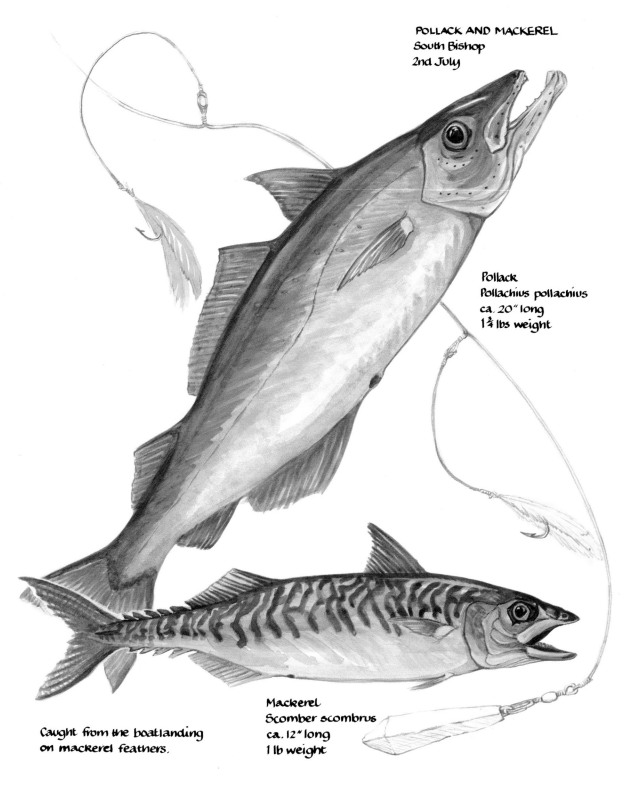

POLLACK AND MACKEREL
South Bishop
2nd July

Pollack
Pollachius pollachius
ca. 20" long
1¾ lbs weight

Mackerel
Scomber scombrus
ca. 12" long
1 lb weight

Caught from the boatlanding
on mackerel feathers.

(Plate 69)

beak, the real danger comes from the edges of its mandibles near to its gape, for these are incredibly sharp, probably to help it grip fish, and its bite leaves a wound not unlike a nick from a razor blade. After we had ringed it we put it on the ground in the yard, where it wandered around like a tiny penguin while I made a few drawings *(Plate 68)*. Eventually we took it down to the boat landing and put it on the rocks a few yards from the gently lapping water. It stood up and shook itself, and then walked solemnly down to the sea and dived in, to re-appear about ten seconds later in the middle of the boat landing, before swimming quickly out to open water.

I collected half a cup of sea-salt crystals today from the evaporated pools in the splash zone on the rocks. They tasted just as good as shop bought ones.

JULY 2nd   When we came on station at the beginning of the month there was an official Trinity House letter waiting for us. This informed us that permission had been granted by the Board to allow the Air Force fighter squadron based at Brawdy to make practice attacks on the lighthouse, using photographic equipment. The attack runs would be at an altitude of approximately 150 feet above sea level, at a speed of 500 miles per hour. The purpose of this advance warning was to let us know what was going on, so that we didn't make an irate radio telephone call of complaint to the Base Commander. Whichever bright spark in the hallowed halls of Trinity House granted permission, he could have had little idea of the effects of his pen stroke. The buildings on South Bishop are only about 120 feet above the water, so for the past few days our afternoons have been shattered by jet fighters hurtling past the living room at eye-level and only fifty feet away! They weren't terribly frequent, but they could make it difficult to get to sleep in the afternoon if we'd been on watch since 4 a.m. We did have some unkind things to say about them, but they didn't seem to mind.

JULY 7th   A change in the weather at last, albeit a slight one. The past week or so has seen more mist and fog patches about reaching a state last night where we had to sound the fog signal. This change has brought a trickle of small migrants, including a magnificent cock whinchat in breeding plumage *(Plate 67)* which hung around in the mist for a couple of hours yesterday. Shearwaters have been attracted to the light in good numbers most nights, and with Pete's help I managed to catch and ring fourteen which crashlanded in the yard. There have been a few more waders about too, with both curlew and common sandpipers passing over calling after dark. Unfortunately one of the oystercatcher chicks has disappeared, probably caught by a large gull despite the vigilance of the adults, although the remaining youngster is doing well, being even more fussed over and fed by both parents!

Relief day. Squally, with some glorious rainshowers at last. While we were   JULY 9th
waiting for the helicopter three grey wagtails landed on the edge of the
rockpools which were rapidly filling with fresh water. They were on their
way south, the autumn migration has started already.

Our scheduled relief yesterday was cancelled due to helicopter trouble, but   AUGUST 7th
everything was back to normal today. We didn't arrive on station until fairly
late, so it was evening before I went out for a look around. There were no
small migrants other than a solitary wheatear, but the tide-race between
South Bishop and Ramsey held a large feeding flock of shearwaters, all
frantically plunge-diving for small fish. I stayed watching them until dusk in
the hope of turning up a stranger, but with no luck. There is every chance of
this feeding flock being a regular feature over the next few days, for the
attraction is largely a function of the state of the tide which concentrates
shoals of sand-eels in the race as they drift south in to St Bride's Bay. On the
flood tide the water pours south over a steep rock step just offshore from the
boat landing and at this point there is a change in the sea level of almost six
feet, as if a great weir had been built across the Sound. The acceleration of
the water over this step is such that small fish are unable to swim against it
and so the sea birds congregate down stream of the step to take advantage
of their helplessness.

Warm and hazy with not much happening, an ideal day to laze around on   AUGUST 8th
the rocks and watch the world go by. There were a few more wheatears
today and a nice male kestrel this morning, but it wasn't until 5.00 p.m. that
the excitement began. I went out to look at the tide race, and found a good
number of shearwaters already feeding with more arriving all the time. It is
very difficult to count birds feeding in such a dense and ever-changing
flock, but they were strung out over a half mile of sea probably 200 yards
wide and I estimated there to be about 20,000 birds. A feeding flock in a tide
race is constantly on the move, for the birds skim low over the sea and
plunge straight below the waves, to re-appear a couple of seconds later. All
the time they are on or in the water the tide race is carrying them south at
seven or eight knots. By the time they lift off to try again, they are a couple
of hundred yards from the focal point of the group, so they fly up tide to
drop in front of the birds on the water. The whole flock is continually 'leap-
frogging' in this way, a sparkling mass of black and white in the low
evening sunlight. There were also about a hundred gannets feeding too,

SHAGS
South Bishop
August

General studies of shags diving
in the boatlanding - the clear
water giving excellent opportunities
for the "underwater" sketches these
were compiled from.

(Plate 70)

SOOTY SHEARWATER
South Bishop
11th August

Slightly more bulky and longer-winged than the
Manx Shearwater, but with a similar way of flying.
Although this one was sooty black, some I have seen
in the past have shown a brown tinge to their plumage.
The silvery-grey underwings are very noticeable.

(Plate 71)

diving arrow-straight into the throng from forty or fifty feet up, to surface seconds later with larger fish snatched from much deeper down. How they managed to see the mackerel through the milling layers of shearwaters and sand-eels I do not know, but they seemed to be unerringly successful. I waited, expecting to see a shearwater killed or maimed by a plunging gannet, but despite the confusion they seemed oblivious to the danger, and I didn't see any injured in this way. They certainly weren't oblivious to the **great skua which came** drifting **purposefully down the tide just after 6.00 p.m.,** for the shearwater ranks parted as he came. He was in search of a meal and his technique for making the shearwaters give up theirs was as effective as it was spectacular. He cruised across the flock ignoring the individual shearwaters which scattered before him, but suddenly accelerated towards a tight bunch of newly-surfaced birds, still settled on the water. Before they could react he smashed bodily into the group forcing them back down into the foam. I saw him grab one shearwater by the neck and shake it so violently that he seemed to be beating the others with one of their companions! The response to this was predictable enough and through my binoculars I could see the scatter of silver particles as the shearwaters all around regurgitated their catches and made a speedy get-away. The skua swam about picking up his spoils, before he did it all again, and in the space of ten minutes he had completed three 'smash and grab' raids and was winging contentedly southwards, leaving the shearwaters still frantically catching sand-eels.

AUGUST 9th

The shearwater feeding flock was rather smaller this evening, but over 200 gannets were diving in the tide race, finding mackerel with ease. There were also a couple of porpoises surfacing repeatedly amongst the shearwaters, and it seemed that the massed shoals of sand-eels were being forced upwards by the mackerel and their predators the porpoises, right into the throngs of seabirds at the surface. I was a bit surprised to see a bull seal swimming across the calm water towards the tide race and assumed him to be joining in the feast of mackerel. His progress was purposeful but not hurried and it took him to a point about thirty yards from the shearwaters, where with his superb swimming skills he was able to briefly maintain a position watching the flock, before he dived steadily, his hind flippers breaking the surface as he went down. A couple of seconds later, he erupted in the middle of a mêlée of shearwaters, scattering them in all directions, but not before he had caught one. Through my binoculars I could clearly see its wings flapping in his mouth. He then shook it violently and swallowed it. I was quite amazed, for I had never counted grey seal among predators of seabirds, but in the next half an hour he caught four more, largely by the same tactics, although he missed on one occasion and only captured the unfortunate shearwater by 'surf-boarding' across the waves in a great shower of foam. The whole scene was greatly reminiscent of television programmes I have seen of Antarctic wildlife, where leopard seals prey on penguins using almost identical surprise tactics and a strikingly similar headshake to despatch their prey.

While all this drama was going on a little group of three oystercatchers landed on the weedy rocks below me. They were two adults and a bird in brown juvenile plumage, this latter wearing a shiny ring. These I presumed to be our resident family, with junior growing at an encouraging rate, even feeding himself now, although one of the parents did open a few mussels to give him a helping beak!

AUGUST 11th Another great skua yesterday evening, but this one didn't stop to feed, much to the relief of the shearwaters. A single heron flew past northwards at dusk, but the feeding flock offshore was still at a moderate level of about 10,000 birds. This evening, however, numbers were dramatically higher and I made a point of being in position well before the turn of the tide, to try and count the groups of shearwaters as they arrived from the south-west. It was fairly easy to start with, little groups of twenty or so joining every couple of minutes, but eventually, after I had something like a thousand counted, I was reduced to estimating how many more were present than my previous figure. By about 7.00 p.m. I began to think that no more had arrived for a little while, and shortly after birds started to leave, so my estimate was pitched at about 40,000 tonight, although it may have been thirty or fifty thousand! There were a number of common terns feeding around the edges of the tide race, diving elegantly to snatch sand-eels from the surface, porpoises were about again, at least six feeding for half an hour before disappearing as mysteriously as they had appeared. The real gem flew close by at 7.15 p.m. in the company of twenty-odd Manx shearwaters. This was slightly larger and sooty-black with silver-grey underwings, a sooty shearwater and one of the treats of autumn in west Wales (*Plate 71*). These birds breed in the southern hemisphere, particularly off the New Zealand coast, and winter in the North Atlantic, during our summer. This one was probably feeding up before heading south in the next couple of weeks. They often show up in ones and twos among feeding flocks of Manx shearwaters, and after severe south-westerly gales good numbers come into the Irish Sea. The real problem is to find the patience needed to sit for hours sorting through thousands upon thousands of the locally breeding Manx shearwaters. Of course, on a lighthouse there is plenty of time to do just that!

AUGUST 15th Tern passage over the last few days has taken over from shearwater feeding flocks as the focus of attention. A slight change in the weather, with cold north-easterly winds and some sea fog, has dispersed the sand-eels and so

STORM PETREL
Hydrobates pelagicus
16th August
Adult ♀

← note pale bar on underwing. (This is obvious in birds in flight.)

winglength: 121 mm
bill length: 11.8 mm
tarsus length: 23.0 mm
weight: 27.6 gms

Picked up dead below the winch cable, had probably been dead a few days. On dissection it showed a swollen oviduct, indication that it is probably a locally breeding bird.

(Plate 72)

the shearwaters are going elsewhere. The bulk of the terns passing by remain unidentified, they are simply too far away to be sure. However, we have had several Arctic terns and a few Sandwich terns amongst the fifty or so common terns that have come close to the rock. The Sandwich terns in particular announce their passing with **persistent** raucous calling, which seems designed to keep the little groups together, individuals on their own look very unsure of themselves!

Although the two great skuas that have gone through southwards lately have ignored the terns completely, one of them did launch a spectacular attack on a two-year-old gannet yesterday, for after the gannet had dived and caught a good-sized fish (I think it was a pollack) the skua chased it for a hundred yards or so, gradually caught up with it and then grabbed the tip of the gannet's right wing in its beak. It then tipped the gannet over in an aerial cartwheeling somersault, at which point the gannet and its breakfast parted company. Before the fish had even hit the water the skua had snatched it from the air, and settled on the sea nearby to eat it in peace. The gannet just seemed somewhat relieved to have got away so lightly and flew off towards the south, no doubt to try for another fish well away from skuas!

AUGUST 16th

I found a dead storm petrel this morning, lying on the rocks below the winch cable. It had a smudge of grease on its breast feathers and I suspect it collided with the cable at night. It was rather high, and must have been killed four or five days ago. Even so I made a page of sketches and drawings then prepared it as a study skin (*Plate 72*). The characteristic odour of petrels proved more persistent than the unsavoury smells of decomposition and after a day or so the skin smelt only of the pleasant, musty 'petrel pong'.

AUGUST 20th

At least one great skua passes each day now and small migrants are becoming increasingly frequent. Willow warblers and wheatears are by far the most numerous but we've had several redstarts and pied flycatchers, mostly wearing the more subdued immature plumage, a sprinkling of spotted flycatchers, grey wagtails and tree pipits. Large numbers of butterflies are around too, with many more coming to the island than previously. Yesterday there were four species, peacocks and red admirals, large whites and small tortoiseshells and at least thirty individuals dotted about, attracted to the white flowers of scurvy-grass or the rotting apples in the rubbish dump. Tern passage continues at a moderate level and although most were only tentatively identified as common/Arctics, a few have come close enough to be specifically identified. The majority of these have been common terns, but a few Arctics and Sandwich terns went by this morning.

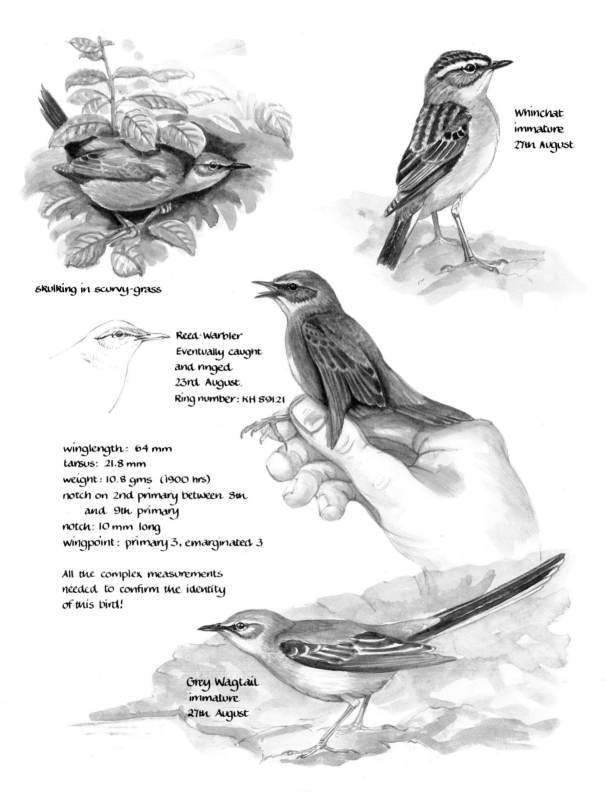

Whinchat
immature
27th August

skulking in scurvy-grass

Reed-Warbler
Eventually caught
and ringed
23rd August.
Ring number: KH 89121

winglength: 64 mm
tarsus: 21.8 mm
weight: 10.8 gms (1900 hrs)
notch on 2nd primary between 8th
     and 9th primary
notch: 10 mm long
wingpoint: primary 3, emarginated 3

All the complex measurements
needed to confirm the identity
of this bird!

Grey Wagtail
immature
27th August

(Plate 73)

REDBACKED SHRIKE
South Bishop
26th August
immature

This bird spent most of the day around the rocks, and evaded all attempts at capture.

It was bold and aggressive and killed an immature Pied Flycatcher, leaving me with the wings and tail as a souvenir!

(Plate 74)

A dozen purple sandpipers were down by the boat landing at dusk, the first I have seen on the rock since the spring. With their breeding grounds on Arctic tundra few people get the chance to see them in the spangled browns and reds of their breeding plumage, but a few of this group were like that, and I assumed them to be post-breeding adults, while the more familiar blue-grey ones I considered to have been youngsters hatched this year.

AUGUST 22nd

A mystery this morning, for there had been a small arrival of migrants over night, including a dozen or more willow warblers and almost as many pied and spotted flycatchers. The rough tangle of scurvy-grass stems attracted several of the small warblers to hunt for insects and from the steps leading down to the boat landing I had a grand view of their comings and goings. A couple of streaky young sedge warblers were skulking among the denser patches, and I kept getting glimpses of another bird of similar size, but a plain, unstreaked rufous-buff colour. It never gave me a complete view of itself, but by evening I had come to the conclusion that it must be either a reed or marsh warbler *(Plate 73)*. I rather hope it will be around tomorrow, for to resolve the question of its identity it would be helpful to examine it in the hand.

AUGUST 23rd

Our strange warbler was still around this morning so I put up a mist net and after half an hour or so succeeded in catching it. An immature reed warbler, the first for South Bishop and an uncommon bird in west Wales. After a comprehensive series of measurements, and ringing, it was released and made straight for the thickest patch of scurvy-grass. Later in the morning it was feeding among the rough herbage by the shed and came out of cover to join a group of willow and sedge warblers who were catching small flies around the rubbish tip. It seems strange that a bird which is so common in eastern England, breeding in practically every reed-filled dyke, should be uncommon, and even quite exciting, on the west coast.

It was overcast and slightly squally this evening and after dark I went round the yard to check the weather. There was a sudden furtive movement under the bench next to the wall and when I investigated further I found a young swift a bit dazed and confused. It seemed unharmed so I put it in a bag and kept it overnight, to be released after ringing the next morning. It must have collided with the aerial wires and fallen into the yard where, because of their short legs and long wings they are unable to take off from level ground. Some must die if they don't get a helping hand from a friendly lightkeeper now and then.

There was a single immature pied flycatcher around the rocks this morning, but by mid-morning it had been killed and partially eaten by a spectacular visitor. Pete first drew my attention to a small bird about the size of a starling which was perched on the winch cable, but it was several minutes before we got a good enough view of it to confirm its identity as an immature red-backed shrike, resplendent in its tiger-striped plumage (*Plate 74*). We spent most of the afternoon watching this superb bird and I was rather surprised when it caught and killed an apparently healthy flycatcher which was almost as large as itself. We made an abortive attempt to catch it but it seemed very alert and well able to avoid a mist net, so in desperation I tried to sneak up behind the wall and drop a net over it, but with a flick of its tail it side-stepped my clumsy efforts, and flitted away over the rocks. We gave up trying to catch it and I concentrated on sketches and notes during the afternoon. I have seen them in west Wales before on autumn migration, particularly on Skokholm Island, but they are infrequent visitors and with the British breeding population diminishing yearly, it's likely that most of these are continental birds which have drifted off-course under the influence of north-easterly winds. After a late tea we went to look for it again, but it was nowhere to be seen. I can only assume that it got tired of being the centre of attention and moved on before dark.

AUGUST 26th

The weather has deteriorated somewhat, with squally showers and north-westerly winds, bringing a noticeable reduction in the numbers of small migrants. Only a wheatear and a pied flycatcher remain, but offshore a number of terns were moving and two great skuas passed through during a squall at midday. A small gull arrived this evening with a group of terns and spent a brief period sitting on the rocks by the helipad. This was an immature little gull (*Plate 67*), superficially rather similar to the kittiwakes nearby, but it carried on south with a party of common terns half an hour later. There were several porpoises off-shore again, some going north and some going south – or was it a group going round and round in circles? This is always the problem with cetaceans around South Bishop and it is often impossible to know just how many are actually passing.

AUGUST 29th

An early relief on a calm and sunny autumn day. When I arrived on shore I found an official letter from Trinity House, notifying me of my transfer from South Bishop to Longships Lighthouse off Land's End in Cornwall. Had I realised that it was my last month, I would have made better use of my time. Over the last eighteen months I have put in nine tours of duty there, and have come to feel very strongly for its own special charm. I shall miss South Bishop very much.

SEPTEMBER 3rd

LONGSHIPS, CORNWALL
50° 04′N; 5° 45′W

(Plate 75)

LONGSHIPS

Longships is everyone's idea of what a lighthouse should be, a slim, granite tower rising from a scatter of jagged rocks a mile to the west of Land's End (*Plate 75*).

This particular stretch of the Cornish coast is one of the most treacherous in Britain and was formerly exploited to its fullest advantage by wreckers. For this reason a light was first exhibited here in September 1795, in a tower designed by architect Samuel Wyatt, and built by Lieutenant Henry Smith under a fifty-year lease granted by Trinity House. In 1836 Trinity House bought out the lessees for £40,676 and took over the running of the station completely. The light exhibited from the first tower was only seventy-nine feet above sea level and during severe storms the lantern was so often under water that the character of the light could not be fixed with any certainty by passing mariners. Eventually in 1875 Wyatt's tower was replaced by the present one, built of grey granite by Sir James Douglass, Trinity House engineer of the day. This current lighthouse is 117 feet high, with a light whose nominal range is nineteen miles. Even so during severe gales waves still crash against the lantern glazing and occasionally dislodge the heavy iron plates from the helipad built on top.

Living on a tower light was a very different experience from being on South Bishop. Space is limited, and everything has to fit precisely into the area provided for it. We slept in curved bunks, on curved mattresses and lived a life of round rooms and spiral staircases. The only real privacy or opportunity to be alone was during middle watch, or in one's bunk behind closed curtains, and there is little doubt that we got on each other's nerves during a month's confinement. I approached my transfer with rather mixed feelings; on the one hand I was looking forward to the experience of living on a 'real' lighthouse, but I knew that it could in no way compare with South Bishop or Coquet for the diversity of wildlife present. I soon found that the only place from which it was possible to birdwatch comfortably was the gallery, although the lantern provided a vantage point in bad weather, when some of the seabird passage was particularly pronounced.

I arrived in Penzance in the early morning of 4 October after travelling overnight from Pembrokeshire. Relief was scheduled for noon on the following day, so the remainder of the day was taken up in arranging overnight accommodation and collecting food. There was a massed gathering of lightkeepers in the bar of the Dolphin Inn at lunchtime, with all the outward-bound crews from the Longships, Wolf Rock, Bishop Rock and Round Island Lighthouse, as well as the crew of the Seven Stones Light Vessel, mustering for relief on the same day. The weather was squally with drizzle and steadily increasing winds forecast for the morrow.

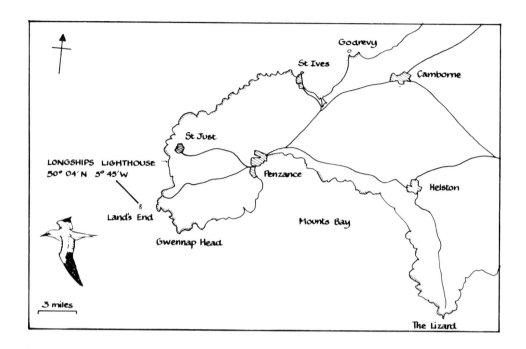

OCTOBER 5th   We arrived on the Longships in blustery conditions, with a force six southerly wind blowing. The helicopter left us on the pad with all our gear and we then had a couple of hours lowering heavy boxes down hatchways and vertical ladders before we were safely ensconced. After tea the customary tour of the station left me marvelling at the ingenuity displayed by designers in fitting so much equipment into small and often odd-shaped spaces. At this time of year days are short and it was already becoming dark when we finally settled down to an evening meal.

OCTOBER 6th   I spent a couple of hours on the gallery this afternoon watching the passage of seabirds southwards. Indeed, all that could be said of the birds I saw was that they passed, for there is no incentive for them to loiter here, and my notes did little more than record numbers and directions of the species involved. It seems likely that the combination of short days and lighthouse routines is going to restrict my birdwatching to either a morning or afternoon session lasting a couple of hours, with no scope for the casual observations made in the course of other jobs which were so typical of other lighthouses. On a tower rock if you aren't actually 'up-top' birdwatching, you are shut inside, with only small windows and thick glass to see through.

There was a substantial passage of auks and gannets this afternoon, with probably a hundred of each passing by. I counted at least a dozen razorbills and six puffins moving south and both Arctic and great skuas, passing very close by the tower. There were in fact two Arctics, one pale-phase and one dark-phase (*Plate 76*). The winds were fairly light south-south-easterly, but the squally conditions had left a long rolling swell which pounded the rocks below the tower ceaselessly.

A morning birdwatch, with showers and increasingly strong winds. Less birds today, although I did count 157 gannets south in an hour, and over fifty auks. A single great skua came by and not long after a Manx shearwater both heading south. It did cross my mind that the shearwater may have been one of 'my' birds from South Bishop, but that's wishful thinking!

OCTOBER 7th

Although gannets and auks still dominate the passage south I had a brief but conclusive view of a sooty shearwater this afternoon. After early fog, the day became sunny and bright, and as I was watching from the gallery I heard the unmistakable 'chissick' of a pied wagtail. It was flying westwards, heading for the Isles of Scilly, and in the next hour I saw another two on the same course.

OCTOBER 9th

There have been up to three grey seals around during the past couple of days but the increasingly strong winds have kept them away from the rocks today, although I did see one swimming in the sea halfway between us and Land's End. The sea was very rough, last night we had a gale of force eight, gusting nine from the south-west and it was amazing to hear the sound of big waves rolling down on us. They hit the base of the tower with a great boom, causing it to sway slightly and tremble. The breaking water roared up the curve of the granite walls and passed over our living room window. In fact the first big wave caught us unawares, for it splashed seawater through the window and into the living room. We quickly closed the heavy shutters and fastened the window, but were able to leave the corresponding window on the lee side of the tower open, for ventilation. The gales brought numbers of seabirds close by the tower and in two hours I counted 171 gannets, 130 kittiwakes and more than 300 auks moving southwards. Many of the kittiwakes were immatures and they were accompanied by two Sandwich terns and a dark-phase Arctic skua.

OCTOBER 12th

SKUAS
Longships s
October

immature
Kittiwake

immature
Arctic Skua

pale phase
Arctic Skua

dark phase
Arctic Skua

Skua passage is daily at this time
of year, with up to a dozen in the
course of a morning. They pass by
rapidly, occasionally harrying the
Kittiwakes.

(Plate 76)

Sooty Shearwater
passing northwards
9th October

Manx Shearwater -
for comparison

Balearic Shearwater
Puffinus puffinus mauretanicus
passing southwards
27th October

Storm Petrels
14th/15th October
feeding close to the tower
after gales

(Plate 77)

OCTOBER 13th   After the rough weather and seabirds, today brought bright sunshine and a steady stream of meadow pipits heading for the Isles of Scilly. They passed by in ones and twos, occasionally a little group of four or five, and during my hour's watch I counted thirty-seven, along with three pied wagtails. There were two purple sandpipers on the rocks below the tower at low tide, picking around among the weed. They must move back to the mainland at high water, for there is no rock exposed above the water then.

OCTOBER 14th   Our roughest night so far last night, with gales force nine and mountainous seas continuing throughout today. No less than nine skuas went past this morning, five Arctic and four great, by far the most I have seen in such a short space of time. There was also a steady passage of gannets, over 250 going south while I watched. The highlight of the day was without a doubt a group of petrels feeding in the crashing surf around the tower, fluttering and swooping to pick up tiny scraps, and even walking on the water at one point (*Plate 77*). They were probably storm petrels but the rough conditions prevented me from identifying all that I saw. At one point over a dozen were visible on the lee of the tower.

OCTOBER 15th   Much calmer today, and bright sunshine. The heavy swell continues, but I had far better views of the petrels today and I was able to confirm them as storm petrels. There were six around the boat-landing steps at low tide and the way they coped with the incredibly rough water left me full of admiration. Although I have ringed hundreds of them at their breeding colonies in Pembrokeshire the past two days have been my first sightings of them at sea.

OCTOBER 16th   Sunny and relatively mild today, with a trickle of visible migration towards the Isles of Scilly. Meadow pipits again in moderate numbers, about a dozen in an hour with two skylarks and also ten or fifteen unidentified passerines, probably finches of some description, but too far away to be certain.

OCTOBER 19th   A bit of a quiet patch lately, but we did have a single great skua going southwards this morning and a little flock of scoter, five common and a nice female velvet, heading for the coast. Gannet passage is picking up a bit again with over a hundred south. It was overcast and misty most of the day and, while we were having lunch at midday, a jackdaw landed on the window sill. It sat there looking through the open window at us and I felt sure it would have come inside had the Principal Keeper not made a hostile move in its direction. It flew off towards the mainland no doubt a little dismayed at its reception.

Another Arctic skua passed on its way south this morning, this time a dark-phase bird. The sea was relatively calm and about a dozen purple sandpipers were feeding on the rocks below the tower. At midday I noticed a tiny grey and white bird on the sea near the boat landing. Through my telescope I watched my first red-necked phalarope for twenty minutes as it swam about feeding (*Plate 78*). It was very agile in the water, turning and pirouetting as it picked tiny creatures from the surface. Like the petrels it seemed incongruous that such a tiny bird should winter at sea through gales and storms, but the phalarope spends the greater part of its life on the ocean, and only comes to boggy pools in the Arctic tundra for the brief breeding season. With the aid of my telescope and tripod I was able to make some sketches before the bird was disturbed by a group of herring gulls and flew off out to sea.

OCTOBER 21st

Several gangs of starlings flew east towards the mainland this morning, and I hoped it would herald the start of a substantial movement, but by 10.30 a.m. it had stopped and only about fifty had gone by. A flock of thirty seaducks came up from the south-east at lunchtime, and as they passed close by the tower I was able to count twenty-nine common scoter and one female scaup (*Plate 79*). They turned away towards the Isles of Scilly and were lost from view in a squally shower. Two grey seals were lying out on the rocks this afternoon, the first I have seen in over a week.

OCTOBER 25th

Very quiet today, but a single Manx shearwater was quite an event, for it wasn't the usual black and white Atlantic form but the dusky brown Balearic race which breeds on the islands of the western Mediterranean. This race occasionally occurs off the south-western coast of Britain and the English Channel in autumn but I had not seen one during my lighthouse service before.

OCTOBER 27th

My birthday, largely spent in standing on the boat landing waiting for the lighthouse tender to land oil and water. She didn't, because the sea was too rough to do so safely at low water. George, the other assistant keeper, showed me a disc of thick glass set into the rock below the tower, which is

OCTOBER 30th

On the sheltered water of the boat landing at mid-day, feeding avidly, spinning and pirovetting in pursuit of macroplankton.

Quite small, only about the size of a starling.

(Plate 78)

SCOTER AND SEADUCK
Longships
October

Long lines of scoter are quite frequent
passing by Longships, and occasionally
other species of duck accompany them.

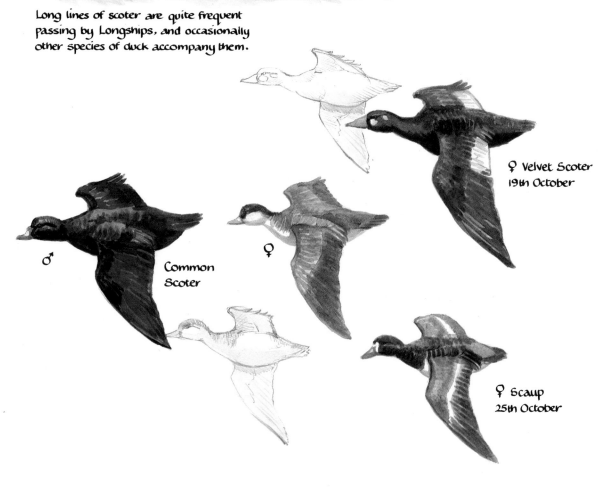

♀ Velvet Scoter
19th October

♂

Common
Scoter

♀

♀ Scaup
25th October

(Plate 79)

fixed in position on a fault line in the rock and acts as an early-warning system. If the rock shifts, the glass cracks. That's the time to abandon lighthouse, for once the glass has cracked, it's a fair bet that the tower will be next. I wasn't too encouraged by the fact that here I was only two days from relief and had only just found this out! Had I known about it I would have been down here every day come hell or high water, checking on that piece of glass! My time on the boat landing was not completely wasted, for a big flock of common scoter went by us, at least sixty-five strong and as we were packing up a female merlin passed by heading south.

NOVEMBER 2nd   Relief day, squally rain showers and winds gusting to gale force. Despite the foul weather we left Longships by helicopter in mid-morning and we were back in Penzance in time to catch the 12.20 p.m. train home.

NOVEMBER 30th   Predictably enough it's relief day so the weather is awful, with squally showers and west south-west gales force eight, gusting nine. All our gear and food was packed and ready, but we waited for most of the morning while decisions were made about the potential hazards of relief by helicopter in such a gale. The road outside the Penzance depot was a foot deep in water and up by the Dolphin Inn I watched half a dozen enterprising turnstones foraging in the gutters, presumably the only alternative being the storm-battered beach. Eventually we were away, at low water, and as we approached the Longships the sea for miles around was white with foam and breakers. The force of the wind on the helipad was unbelievable so we made the transfer of men and equipment in record time and settled down in the safety of the living room. Later that evening as high water approached the waves were breaking on the lantern glazing. It was uncanny the way the roaring of the waves ceased as it passed our window and for a brief moment left us in silence, virtually under water, before cascading down again.

This is, of course, a Christmas tour, we will not be ashore again until just before the New Year and consequently we had all brought a little something extra. I had not imagined that the close proximity of Longships to Land's End would make any difference so I was pleasantly surprised to find an array of extra goodies for us. A local butcher had offered all the lighthouses large turkeys at wholesale prices, so we had clubbed together and paid a paltry sum for a huge bird, which I doubted we could finish. The Penzance Round Table had thoughtfully provided each keeper with a bag containing some paperback books, sweets and chocolate, a large can of beer, a miniature brandy, fruit, nuts, chewing gum and crackers. The most surprising and touching gift was from two elderly ladies in the Midlands, who apparently frequently visited Cornwall on holiday and always made the journey to Land's End to gaze across the water at Longships. For many years they had sent a beautiful Christmas cake to the crew of the Longships, along with a respectable sum 'to allow the keepers to buy some meat for Christmas'! All this was sent to the care of the local vicar in Penzance and passed over to us prior to relief. Being intensely practical, keeping any sort of meat for a long period is difficult on a tower rock and our turkey took up a large part of our fridge space, so we turned the good ladies' contribution into three pieces of prime steak, each one weighing over two pounds and ate them fried this evening as the mountainous seas pounded the tower all around us.

DECEMBER 1st

The rough weather continues and although there was a slight decrease in the wind strength at midday, this evening it had reached a full gale again. Birds were few and far between, one small group of nine common scoter with a female velvet scoter being the only observations worthy of note.

DECEMBER 9th

Ten days of gale force winds finally came to an end last night and the day dawned bright and sunny. All I've seen lately in the way of birds is a few gannets and kittiwakes and the usual gulls, but today there was a respectable passage of auks, with over 100 going south in an hour, a trickle of common gulls off-shore, and a group of a dozen purple sandpipers feeding on the rocks at low tide. Most unexpected were two great northern divers, an adult and an immature, fishing in the boat landing mid-morning (*Plate 80*). They stayed around for about half an hour, but I didn't see them catch anything.

DECEMBER 19th

A prolonged period of moderate winds with squally showers, mist and drizzle. Several more divers have passed by during the last few days, but they have all been too far away to identify with any certainty. I don't think they were great northerns, they seemed to be too small in comparison with other birds nearby. Purple sandpipers and turnstones continue to visit us every day at low water, this morning fifteen or twenty were scattered about the rocks. Best bird of the day was a nice first-winter glaucous gull which stayed around the rocks from 11.00 a.m. until midday. This is the first I have ever seen on the west coast, in direct contrast to my duty on Coquet and St Mary's Island, where they seemed to be around all the time.

GREAT NORTHERN DIVER
Longships
Adult and immature
9th December
Fishing in the boat landing

Glaucous Gull
19th December

Great Skua
20th December

adult

immature

Immature has a chequer pattern on the back,
and more contrasted head and neck.

(Plate 80)

KILLER WHALES
Orca orcinus
21st December

Adult ♂
and probably
an Imm. ♂

First seen coming down from the north,
while we were working on the boatlanding.
They passed by about fifty yards away, the
bull showing pale patches and a tall triangular
dorsal fin.

Adult ♂
ca. 20 feet long
dorsal fin ca. 5 feet tall

Quite magnificent! Totally breathtaking!

(Plate 81)

DECEMBER 20th   After the excitement of the glaucous gull yesterday a great skua turned up this afternoon. This was particularly unexpected, because I had always imagined them to be summer visitors to their high-latitude breeding grounds and certainly my observations on South Bishop and Longships this autumn has indicated a very strong passage south. This bird followed the general trend and flew away southwards until lost from sight.

DECEMBER 21st   THV *Stella* arrived off station today and we spent some time on the landing taking on oil and water. There was a moderate swell running and we had reached a lull in the proceedings by 11.00 a.m. when I noticed two cetaceans coming down the tide towards us on a course which would bring them fairly close by the rocks where we stood (*Plate 81*). They were blowing regularly and I imagined them to be either pilot or bottle-nosed whales, but as they came closer I could see that the larger of the two had a tall triangular dorsal fin and his companion a triangular fin only slightly smaller. This rang a mental bell and as they passed I could clearly see whitish patches on their flanks and heads which confirmed them as killer whales. They were past us in a few minutes, but they remain one of the most impressive sights of my lighthouse service, the more so as they are only infrequently recorded off south-western Britain. Most records are in the southern Irish Sea and the west coast of Ireland and Scotland. They are migratory, moving down the eastern Atlantic coast in late summer and autumn, and moving off-shore as winter approaches.

DECEMBER 25th   The only bird of any consequence today was our turkey, which was surrounded by a vast array of vegetables to make our Christmas dinner. It was the most massive feast I have ever eaten and I felt little inclined to do any birdwatching after it, the more so as the weather was uninviting, cold and drizzling, although not windy.

DECEMBER 29th   A calm and sunny day, the helicopter took us ashore at 11.00 a.m. and as we flew over the mainland between Land's End and Penzance we saw two foxes, out for a stroll in the frosted fields. It was a bit of a rush to catch the midday train, but I made it and settled down to eat my way through a pile of turkey sandwiches, brought from Longships and made for the journey.

We were fortunate to get out to Longships despite the rough weather this JANUARY 25th
morning, for it steadily deteriorated this afternoon, into a severe south-
westerly gale. Through patchy showers we could see huge rollers sweeping
in from the Atlantic to smash unimpeded onto the rocks below us.
Surprisingly a seal was swimming about in the foaming water and I am sure
that it was playing, enjoying the experience of surfing along on the crest of
the biggest waves. Eventually it drifted away to the north-east, but for a
while I could still see it popping up in the troughs between the breakers.

The high tide last night produced some of the strongest waves I have JANUARY 26th
experienced on Longships. The whole tower shook and trembled all night
as waves surged right up and over the helipad. This morning a slight
decrease in the wind revealed that a large piece of the masonry from the
north boat landing has been smashed away by the force of the water, and
that the helicopter pad did not escape unscathed. We climbed out onto the
pad to inspect the damage and found two of the huge cast metal plates had
been broken away from their anchorage points. The force of the water had
lifted them away from their position and left them hanging in the safety net
around the pad. It took two of us to lift them back into place, an operation
which required us to stand with one foot on the pad and the other on a
narrow girder, with a sheer drop of 120 feet between our legs! A small price
to pay, for if more than a couple of plates are missing, it is impossible for the
helicopter to land, and our next relief would have to be by boat, and would
be very dependent on the weather.

Birds are very few and far between these days, only an odd gull or auk to JANUARY 27th
break the monotony, so I was pleased to see yet another **winter great skua**
this morning, going south just after dawn.

As so often happens the gales are followed by a period of calmer weather. JANUARY 30th
There was an immature drake eider on the sea this morning and a sizable
mixed flock of turnstones and purple sandpipers, at least thirty feeding
among the rocks. The local fishermen who handline for mackerel from small
boats had some powerful competition today, in the shape of a fleet of purse-
seiners, many of which are converted trawlers from the north-east, where
unemployment and the decline of the fishing industry has meant large and
modern ships being laid up if there is no mackerel fishing to be had. At least
a part of the problem could be seen in the shape of a large Russian factory

Gannets take several years to reach adult plumage, and blotchy individuals are common. These little sketches show some of the variation.

Razorbills

Puffin

Guillemots

Passage of auks is particularly marked in rough weather, and at sea can be difficult to identify.

(Plate 82)

ship prevented by law from fishing inside British waters, buying catches from local boats. Beyond the three-mile limit East European boats are rapidly cleaning up the sea with factory-fishing methods which make me wonder if there is any future for our marine environment.

Squally showers, fog patches and gales sum up the week gone by. Auks and FEBRUARY 11th gannets have reappeared in some numbers lately (*Plate 82*), this afternoon 150 gannets were diving for fish between Longships and the mainland, and one enterprising local from Sennen Cove made a respectable catch of mackerel on handlines amid the plummeting gannets. The auks must have been feeding on smaller fry, possibly sprats, I don't think they could cope with mackerel.

The bad weather continues but auks and gannets feed around the tower FEBRUARY 18th every day now, surely an indication of the massive concentrations of mackerel and other fish in this area. The rough seas have kept the fishing fleet well away from the coast, but yesterday morning a submarine passed us heading out to sea. The Admiralty Chart shows the area off Longships as a submarine training ground, but this is the first one I have seen in spite of all the time I have spent in gazing out to sea!

The Trinity House helicopter brought an electrician and a plumber on FEBRUARY 21st station this morning, so that they can carry out some repairs and go ashore with us on relief tomorrow. The weather forecast is favourable, at long last the persistent squally weather, which has lasted over two weeks, is set to change.

The helicopter took us off Longships at 10.15 a.m. and before too long I was FEBRUARY 22nd on the railway station in Penzance, waiting for the midday train, little realising that I had left Longships for the last time, and would not be returning.

POSTSCRIPT

When I first joined Trinity House one of the main reasons for becoming a lightkeeper was the opportunity it provided for the study of natural history, particularly seabirds and migration. In this respect South Bishop, in my home county of Pembrokeshire, was the high point of my career. Over the past months it had become apparent to me that natural history was the most important aspect of my life and I had decided to seek a career opening which would develop this interest. In early March I was offered a seasonal job as warden of a bird observatory and nature reserve in southern England, which I felt would be a useful rung on the ladder. I resigned from the lighthouse service in late March and took up my new post on 1 April, at the start of the spring migration.

INDEX

Italic folios refer to illustrations

auk, little, 64, *66*
avocet, 86, *87*

blackbird, 42, 49, 68, 73, 83, 129, 132, 133, 136, *138*, 144, 145
blackcap, 132, 152, 156
brambling, 73, 123, 125
bream, Ray's, 31, *33*, 59
brimstone butterfly, 90
bunting, snow, 68, 123, 125, *126*
butterfish, 35
buzzard, rough-legged, 83, *84*

chaffinch, 48, 125, 152
chiffchaff, 10, 11, 83, 86, 95, *97*, 98, 102, 118, 125, 129, 149, 152, 158
cod, *58*
codling, 31, 38
coley, 31, 38
coot, 78
Coquet, 15, 18, 25–49, 52, 54, 90, 179, 189
cormorant, 44, 60
coypu, 82, 86
crab: green shore, 35
velvet swimming, 35, *37*
crawfish, *113*, 114
Cromer, 17, 70–91
curlew, 9, 35, 38, 42, 43, 54, 65, *67*, 82, 102, 152, 166

dipper, 83, *88*
diver: black-throated, 47
great northern, 44, 189, *190*
red-throated, 38, 44, 65

dogfish, 31, *74*, 114
dolphin, Risso's, 105–6, *109*
dove: collared, 152, 158
turtle, 102, *150*, 159
duck, tufted, 59, 61, 78
dunlin, 9, 31, 42, 45, 54, *56*, 147, 156

eel: conger, 31
sand-, 167, 170, 171
eider, 27, 30, 31, 34, 35, *36*, 38, 42, 48, 49, 57, 65, 193

fieldfare, 49, 73, 86, *130*, 132, *138*, 145
firecrest, *88*, 90
flamingo, Chilean, 61, *63*
flycatcher: pied, *150*, 152, *153*, 173, 176, 177
red-breasted, 122, *124*
spotted, 11, 95, *97*, 103, 118, *153*, 173, 176
fulmar, 44, 82, *85*, 90, 137, *143*, 145

gadwall, 76, 78
gannet, *74*, 103, 105, 136, 137, *143*, 144, 156, 163, 167, 170, 173, 181, 184, 189 *194*, 195
godwit: bar-tailed, 65
black-tailed, 76, *77*
goldcrest, 10, 82, 118, 122, 149, 152, 158
goldeneye, 35, *39*, 53, 57, 59, 68
goldfinch, 42, 45, 48–9, 152
goose: Brent, 78
Egyptian, *81*, 82
greylag, 78
greenfinch, 125, 136, 140, 144, 147
greenshank, *89*, 90
guillemot, 45, 57, 60, 64, 65, 73, 99, 137,

guillemot: *cont*.
  157, 163, *165*, 166, *194*
gull: black-headed, *79*
  common, 47, 68, *79*, 147, 189
  glaucous, *29*, 30, 31, 40, 42, 44, 47, 49,
    55, 59, 68, 189, *190*, 192
  great black-backed, 28, 30, 40, *41*, 98,
    137
  herring, 28, 31, 44, 76, 98, 99, 102,
    123, 137, *160*, 162
  lesser black-backed, 12, 147
  little, *161*, 177
gunnel, 64

harrier, hen, 78
heron, grey, 61, 106, 117, 171
hummingbird hawk moth, 163

jackdaw, 83, 123, 125, 133, 140, 148,
  184–5

kelp, *46*, 47
kestrel, 68, 167
kingfisher, 78, *81*
kittiwake, 47, 60, 76, 106, 119, *120*, 136,
  137, 139, 156, 177, 181, *182*, 189
knot, 38, 42, 54, *55*, 61

ladybird, seven-spot, *112*
lapwing, 49, 76, *142*, 144
large white butterfly, 110, 163, 173
linnet, 90, 119, 149, 152
Longships, 15, 16, 18, 178–95
lumpsuckers, 31, *33*

mackerel, *164*
magpie, 129
magpie moth, 110, *112*
mallard, 59, 61, 76
martin: house, 90, 102, 119, 122, 154,
    158
  sand, 86, 90, 102
merganser, red-breasted, 35, *39*, 53, 78
merlin, 30–1, 40, 43, *151*, 152, 188
moorhen, 76, 132, *135*
mussels, horse, 35, 53

owl: long-eared, 154, *155*

  short-eared, 10, 59–60, 61, 64, 152, 154
oystercatcher, 30, *32*, 43, 54, 98–9, 159,
  160, 162, 166, 171

painted lady butterfly, 163
partridge, red-legged, 73, *75*, 76
peacock butterfly, 90, 110, *112*, 173
peregrine, 106, 119, *121*, 123, 136, 148
petrel, storm, 114, *115*, 116, 117, *172*,
  173, *183*, 184, 195
phalarope, red-necked, 185, *186*
pintail, 59, 73, *74*
pipefish, greater, 73, *74*, 83
pipit: meadow, 11, 30–1, 49, 145, 147,
    148, 149, *153*, 184
  rock, 105, *108*, 140
  tree, *153*, 154, 173
plover: golden, 76, 78, *80*, 90, 145
  grey, 38, 43, 48
  ringed, 30, 42, 43, 54, *55*, *56*, 156
pochard, 59, 78
pollack, 114, *164*
porpoise, common, 105, *109*, 140, 156,
  162, 170, 171, 177
puffin, 65, *66*, 149, *157*, 181, *194*

rabbit, 47–8
raven, *128*, 132–3, 148
razorbill, 64, 99, 137, *157*, 181, *194*
red admiral butterfly, 163, 173
redpoll, 152
redshank, *8*, 40, 42, 43, 44, 78, 136, 140
  spotted, *89*, 90
redstart, 11, 118, *150*, 152, *153*, 154, 158,
    173
  black, 82, 123, *126*
redwing, 68, 73, 123, *127*, 129, 132, *138*,
  140, 144, 145, 147
ring ouzel, 86, *88*, 90
robin, 44, 45, 49, 83, 152
rock sea spurrey, *101*
rockling, five-bearded, *58*
rook, 123, 125, 133, 140, 148

St Mary's Island, 16, 17, 21, 50–69, 189
sanderling, 54, *55*, 72
sandhopper, 38

sandpiper: common, 156, 166
  purple, *8*, 30, 31, 35, 38, 40, 41–3, 44,
    45, 48, 54, 64, 156, 176, 184, 185,
    189, 193
scaup, 185, *187*
scoter: common, *39*, 57, 59, 136, 140,
    149, 184, 185, *187*, 188, 189
  velvet, 184, *187*, 189
scurvey-grass, common, *101*
sea-anemone, 35
sea fir, 35
sea urchin, 35
seal, grey, 60, 65, 110, *112*, 140, *141*, 149,
    170–1, 181, 193
shag, 38, 44, 57, 60, *62*, 137, *168*
shearwater: Balearic, *183*
  Cory's, *143*, 145
  great, 103, 105, *107*
  Manx, 9, 10, 11, 98, 99, *100*, 102, 103,
    107, 110, 114, 116, 117, 145, 148,
    149, 154, 156, 166, 167, 170, 171,
    173, 181, *183*, 185
  sooty, *169*, 171, 181, *183*
shelduck, 65, 76
shoveler, 76, 86
shrew, water, 83, *84*
shrike, red-backed, *174*, 177
shrimp, common, 35, *37*
siskin, *142*, 144
skua: Arctic, 118, 119, *120*, 181, *182*, 184,
    185
  great, 122, 170, 171, 173, 177, 181, *182*,
    184, *190*, 192, 193
skylark, 40, 42, 123, 125, 132, *134*, 147,
    184
small tortoiseshell butterfly, 90, 173
snipe, 78, 132, *136*
South Bishop, 9–11, 15, 16, 17, 18, 19,
    20, 21, 22, 92–177, 179, 196
sparrow, tree, 102, 103
starling, 49, 73, 106, 123, 125, 129, 132,
    133, *134*, 136, 145, 185
stonechat, 145, *146*, 148
sunfish, 106, 110, *111*
swallow, 86, 90, 102, 119, 122, 152, 154,
    158
swan: Bewick's, 78
  mute, 59

  whooper, 59, 61, 78
swift, 103, *104*, 116, 163, 176

teal, 59, 65, 76, 78
tern: Arctic, 118, 119, 173
  common, 118, 119, 171, 173, 177
  Sandwich, 86, 90, *91*, 119, 173, 181
thrift, *101*
thrush, song, 45, 49, 60, 123, 129, 132,
    133, *138*, 144, *146*, 147
tick, castor bean, *146*, 147
tit, bearded, 76
trigger fish, spotted, 65, 68, *69*
turnstone, *8*, 30, 31, 35, 38, 40, 42, 43,
    45, 54, 110, 156, 188, 189, 193

wagtail: grey, 57, 59, 167, 173, *175*
  pied, 119, 145, 149, *150*, 181, 184
  white, 149, *150*
  yellow, 90
warbler: grasshopper, 11, 95, *97*, 117,
    118, 154, 156, 158
  reed, *175*, 176
  sedge, 10, 11, 95, *97*, 110, 117, 118,
    152, *153*, 156, 158, 176
  willow, 10, 86, 95, *97*, 98, 102, 110,
    118, 149, 152, 156, 158, 173, 176
water rail, *130*, 132, 133
whale, killer, *191*, 192
wheatear, 10, 11, 82, 83, 86, 90, 98, *101*,
    102, 118, *121*, 122, 149, 152, 154, 156
whelk, common, 35, *37*
whimbrel, 9, 102, 118, *151*, 152, 156
whinchat, *161*, 166, *175*
whitethroat, 10, 95, 102, 156, 158
wigeon, 59, 65, 76, 78, 86
woodcock, *131*, 132, 133
woodpecker, green, 76
woodpigeon, 30, 125, 147, 156
wrack: bladder, 35, *37*
  egg, 35, *37*
  horn, 73
  serrated, 35, *37*
wren, 42, 44, 45, 122, 123, *124*, 149

yellow underwing moth, *112*